Merry Christmas, Sarah

Thanks for allowing me to design and build a 401K for your employees. And thanks for your friendship.

It's a joy to serve you & to work with you.

PRAISE FOR REPURPOSEMENT

"In Repurposement, Troy Redstone has tackled one of the most pervasive and most ignored crises facing our nation today. Using relatable language and touching personal anecdotes, Troy is able to help us examine retirement in an unexpected and powerful new way."

—DR. DANIEL CROSBY, AUTHOR OF *THE LAWS OF WEALTH* AND *THE BEHAVIORAL INVESTOR*

"Repurposement is about achieving a timely and dignified retirement that requires a thoughtful and proactive approach to establishing goals and maximizing preretirement savings. Engaging an experienced retirement planning professional is the best way to ensure your path is realistic and that you stay on course."

—JASON C. ROBERTS, ERISA COUNSEL, CEO, PENSION RESOURCE INSTITUTE; PARTNER, RETIREMENT LAW GROUP

"We live in vision or we live in circumstance. This incredible book by Troy helps us take a look at the circumstance of retiring and having the vision of making the following years the best years. With all the years of living and learning, why waste it and just live without purpose? I use a phrase often: So what…now what? This book teaches 'So what…? You retired. Now what? Be a blessing and make a difference.'"

—DR. KEVIN ELKO, AUTHOR OF *THE SENDER*, *TRUE GREATNESS*, AND *THE PEP TALK*

"So many people think retirement is the end, when, in fact, it truly is a beautiful reset. Troy's mission to help people redefine retirement is as refreshing as it is necessary. By helping people look past the math, Repurposement sets the stage for a meaningful transition to retirement."

—PETER DUNN (PETE THE PLANNER®), *USA TODAY* MONEY COLUMNIST AND AUTHOR OF 10 BOOKS

"Troy hits upon one of the key aspects of retirement: 'What do I do with my time and resources postretirement?' His idea of Repurposement is unique and positions the readers to positively reconsider what life can be post-working career."

—JAMES D. ROBISON, AIF®, FOUNDER, WHITE OAK ADVISORS; PLANADVISER'S TOP 100 RETIREMENT PLAN ADVISERS, 2013, 2015, 2017

PRAISE FOR 401(K) ARCHITECTURE

"If you lead a purpose-driven business intent on being a good corporate citizen, this book can help with employee benefits that serve all three goals: your people, your purpose, and your profit. It breaks down the 'benefit of benefits' and helps business leaders identify the ROI of investing in the company 401(k)."

—DR. DANIEL CROSBY, AUTHOR OF *THE LAWS OF WEALTH* AND *THE BEHAVIORAL INVESTOR*

"Those who oversee workplace retirement plans like 401(k)s are entrusted with an awesome responsibility—what some courts have described as the highest standards known to law. Too many are asked to do so without any background or training. 401(k) Architecture provides that much-needed roadmap that can not only help those new to the role get a solid grounding but expand and enhance the focus of those who have been in that role for some time."

—NEVIN ADAMS, JD, CHIEF CONTENT OFFICER, AMERICAN RETIREMENT ASSOCIATION

"The themes introduced and explained in 401(k) Architecture are highly relevant given the impact of the COVID-19 pandemic and include robust discussions on the use of Behavioral Economics and science to achieve successful outcomes for employees. Redstone clearly and comprehensively makes the retirement plan case for any purpose-driven leader who genuinely cares about their employees' performance, well-being, and financial security."

—JOHN SULLIVAN, EDITOR IN CHIEF,
401(K) SPECIALIST MAGAZINE

"401(k) Architecture offers an insightful road map for how employers can effectively design and properly govern their retirement programs. Redstone explores creative, flexible, and innovative strategies for long-term and sustainable retirement plan building. It's a common-sense, tactical-to-practical roadmap for any retirement Plan Sponsor struggling to navigate the complex world of 401(k) plans."

—SAM HENSON, JD, DIRECTOR OF LEGISLATIVE/
REGULATORY AFFAIRS, LOCKTON; PRESIDENT,
INTERNATIONAL SOCIETY OF CEBS®

"A company culture in which employees can feel appreciated will do more than any amount of compensation to engage the workforce. 401(k) Architecture gives readers the tools they need to convey their outstanding commitment to the workforce in the design of the retirement benefits program. Recommended reading for CFOs, HROs, business owners, *and Plan Administrators seeking to achieve extraordinary business outcomes."*

—ERIC HENON, PRESIDENT, EACH ENTERPRISE, LLC;
EXECUTIVE DIRECTOR, RETIREMENT ADVISOR COUNCIL

"As an employee benefits attorney now entering my 31st year of practice, I have worked with many Investment Advisors and specialized retirement plan consultants. However, in my many years of working with Troy on various professional matters, what has always made Troy unique is his ability to be authentic and relatable to his audience, whether that is with a group of line workers in the breakroom or C-suite executives in the boardroom. He is also a creative thinker and innovative in his concepts; he was espousing the merits of financial wellness in a retirement plan long before other competitors. Troy brought that same level of innovation and authenticity to his first book, Repurposement, and it is here again in his next installment, 401(k) Architecture. A reader of either book will come away with a renewed sense of understanding of not just the importance of 401(k) investing, but why it is critically important to each of our lives."

—BRIAN JOHNSTON, JD, ERISA COUNSEL,
JACKSON LEWIS, PC

"In 401(k) Architecture, Troy Redstone shares his expertise in 401(k) plan design, showing you proven methods from Behavioral Economics to structure your retirement plan to lead your employees to invest even more into their own financial well-

being. This is a must-read for business leaders who value their employees and want their business to grow."

—TED MITCHELL, JD, PRINCIPAL, HAYNES BENEFITS, PC

"Troy Redstone is a good man who cares deeply about 401(k) plan participants and their retirement. I'm excited to read this book."

—BRANDON LONG, JD, ERISA COUNSEL, MCAFEE & TAFT

"Troy Redstone combines practical applications from Behavioral Finance and Behavioral Economics with real-world plan consulting and advisory experience and expertise. A thought-leader in the industry, Troy is passionate about helping every employee reach the work-life finish line with a successful retirement outcome. His experience is significant and lends a level of thoughtful credibility few others in our industry match."

—JAMES D. ROBISON, MANAGING DIRECTOR, STRATEGIC RETIREMENT PARTNERS; PLANADVISER'S TOP 100 RETIREMENT PLAN ADVISERS, 2015, 2017, 2019, 2020

"Troy Redstone demonstrates in 401(k) Architecture the rare combination of subject matter expertise with engaging and relatable application. The stories from other business leaders are encouraging and inspiring, but then the roadmap on how to design a successful retirement plan provides a great game plan for success."

—GLENN WADDELL, JD, GENERAL COUNSEL AND CHIEF COMPLIANCE OFFICER, EVERSOURCE WEALTH ADVISORS®, LLC

"A must-read book, 401(k) Architecture is about the behavior of people to create and participate in investment tools to prepare them for retirement. I am of the age where retirement is rapidly approaching, so I pay attention to 401(k) and investment strategies more than ever. Troy is dedicated to helping employers prepare their employees for a better, more comfortable retirement."

—MARVIN CAROLINA, PRESIDENT,
BETTER BUSINESS BUREAU

"401(k) Architecture is about the profound choices fiduciaries make that will shape and determine the retirement outcomes for their employees over the next 10, 20, and 30 years or more. It's a high calling and heavy responsibility that requires purpose and passion. I'd recommend the book for anyone responsible for their company retirement plan. The interviews with business leaders—talking about how they practice the principles they espouse—were especially inspiring. It all adds up to a highly enjoyable and uplifting read."

—JOSH ITZOE, CFP®, AIF®, FOUNDER AND CEO,
FIDUCIARYWOR(K)S; AUTHOR OF *FIXING THE 401(K)* AND *THE FIDUCIARY FORMULA*

"For Plan Sponsors looking to make their plan a valued benefit instead of a 'nice to have,' Troy is a respected source in our industry with vast experience!"

—COURTENAY SHIPLEY, CRPS®, CPFA®,
RETIREMENT PLANOLOGY, INC.

"Troy has done an excellent job blending basic retirement plan knowledge with bursts of new ideas, concepts, and perspectives. This book is a perfect read for anyone new to running a retirement plan and the seasoned pros."

—JEANNE FISHER, CFP®, CPFA®, #401KLADY, MANAGING DIRECTOR, STRATEGIC RETIREMENT PARTNERS

"Troy Redstone covers the landscape with respect to what every employer should be considering when creating and operating its 401(k) plan. Applying his knowledge of Behavioral Finance and Behavioral Economics and his real-world experience and expertise with 401(k) plans, in 401(k) Architecture, Troy provides a solid framework for employers wanting to do the best job they can when it comes to 401(k) plan sponsorship and helping every employee reach the finish line with a successful retirement outcome."

—PHIL MCKNIGHT, JD, PARTNER, STINSON LLP

"Troy Redstone blends behavioral science and decades of experience serving 401(k) plans to design and build healthy retirement plans aimed at producing healthy retirement outcomes. His first book, Repurposement, was written for employees inside those plans, and now he's written a companion book, 401(k) Architecture, for the employers who sponsor the plans."

—BRAD SCHLOZMAN, JD, ERISA COUNSEL, HINKLE LAW FIRM, LLC

"*401(k) Architecture provides the nuts and bolts of how to design and build a successful retirement plan for your employees. If providing top-notch benefits and taking care of your employees is a value for your company, this book provides practical resources to help you take the necessary steps.*"

—DANA DREIER, CPA, SENIOR MANAGER, CBIZ AND MAYER HOFFMAN MCCANN PC

"*401(k) Architecture offers powerful insights on the direct correlation between the personal and professional lives of individuals and how companies that recognize these realities and take action will not only survive but thrive. Troy views history through the lens of a thought-leader in the retirement industry to create a roadmap for purpose-driven benefits that will stand the test of time.*"

—JASON KEY, VP, HEAD OF CONSULTANT RELATIONS, RETIREMENT PLAN SERVICES, LINCOLN FINANCIAL GROUP

401(k) ARCHITECTURE

Design a Retirement Plan That Serves Your Purpose *and* Your People

Troy Redstone

MAHOUT PRESS

COPYRIGHT © 2021 TROY REDSTONE
All rights reserved.

401(K) ARCHITECTURE
Design a Retirement Plan That Serves Your Purpose and Your People

ISBN   978-1-5445-2468-9 *Hardcover*
        978-1-5445-2467-2 *Paperback*
        978-1-5445-2466-5 *Ebook*

Cover design by Michael Nagin
Author photo by Linsey McAfee

*To my amazing bride, Kristalynn,
forever and ever. Amen.*

*And to the retirement plan professionals
who continue to raise the bar.
I am humbled to be part of the "fraternity"
of professional retirement plan advisors,
subject matter experts, "ERISA Geeks,"
and Plan Fiduciary Advisors.*

*This book is a simple guide to building
a workplace retirement plan that works,
and it is dedicated to the countless employers
who really care about their people
and strive to reward loyal employees
with successful retirement outcomes.*

Like you! :)

CONTENTS

FOREWORD 17
PREFACE 21

WHY

1. SECRET TO SUCCESS 33
2. 401(K) AS THE CORNERSTONE 65
3. REPURPOSEMENT 83

HOW

4. DESIGNING HEALTHY PLANS 105
5. MITIGATING RISK 117
6. HIRING THE RIGHT ARCHITECT 133
7. POURING THE FOUNDATION 149
8. PLAN FEES 163
9. KEEP IT SIMPLE 179
10. PLAN DESIGN 101 197
11. FINANCIAL WELLNESS 219

CONCLUSION 237
ACKNOWLEDGMENTS 253
ABOUT THE AUTHOR 255
REFERENCES 257

FOREWORD

As Peter Drucker so famously said, culture really does eat strategy for lunch. We can have the greatest business plan, products, and brand in the world, but if our team members' hearts are not in it, your business will not be successful over the long term.

I have been blessed to lead private and governmental organizations for over 25 years. During this time, I have witnessed all types of cultures. Some leaders believe their employees are lucky to work for them and are replaceable at any time. Some leaders say they value their employees but do not actually show it with their actions. The very best leaders match their words with their actions and show their employees how valuable they are.

I was given the opportunity to buy Regent Bank in the fall

of 2007, and we purchased it on April 1, 2008. My singular goal was to create the best place to work for our employees. I learned that developing a great culture requires true commitment—you can't just talk the talk; you must walk the walk.

At Regent Bank, our board of directors has allowed us to be very generous. We have high expectations for our employees, and they must live our core values every day, but we made a decision to share in the wealth we were creating. We do this through a variety of employee programs, including profit-sharing programs, cash bonuses as we hit certain growth milestones, and extra rewards for going above and beyond as they serve our internal and external clients. We offer financial assistance for employees who have experienced unexpected financial challenges, and, through Troy, we offer a financial wellness program.

The results have been remarkable. Regent Bank has averaged 43% asset growth for seven years in a row, and our stock price has appreciated by 27% per year. During the recent COVID pandemic, our employee morale remained high, and we increased earnings by 41%.

I met Troy Redstone several years ago at a community event in Tulsa, Oklahoma, and we hit it off immediately. I could tell early in our relationship that we were like-minded and Troy was motivated by much more than money—he sincerely wants to make people's lives better.

The book you are about to read is not just a "feel-good" story about making employees happy. It is a win-win strategy in which employees are more satisfied, and they create a stronger, more profitable organization. Addressing the financial lives of our employees through employee benefits (retirement plans and financial wellness programs) will ultimately benefit not just those employees but our businesses as well.

SEAN KOUPLEN

SECRETARY OF COMMERCE AND WORKFORCE DEVELOPMENT

STATE OF OKLAHOMA

CHAIRMAN AND CEO

REGENT BANK

PREFACE

WHO SHOULD READ THIS BOOK...AND WHY?

This book was written for business leaders who want to be successful and employers who care deeply about their people and how these two are the same. Some employers value human resources as a company's most valuable asset. At those companies, employees matter, and management really cares.

401(k) Architecture involves what Behavioral Economists call "choice architecture." It starts with the choice to invest in the workplace retirement plan, and it incorporates a lot of behavioral science to help employees make choices that lead to successful outcomes. This book discusses the correlation between a company's purpose and purpose-driven benefits to take care of our people. It addresses the ROI of investing in employee benefits. And it helps business leaders with a step-by-step roadmap on how to design and build a successful retirement plan.

Many employers care for their employees and strive to improve company culture, to reward those who keep the presses running and keep the lights on. Even the lowest-paid worker in some places is so much more than just a paycheck. This book will demonstrate that (a) it is worth the investment to give them a 401(k) plan that works, (b) it may not cost as much as you think, (c) it will cost more to not invest in Retirement Readiness, and (d) it is truly the path for successful business outcomes.

I will start with the fourth point, drawn from a series of interviews over the last year. By no means are the interviews a large enough sample to draw conclusive data in terms of a research project, but the themes were undeniable. I randomly selected business leaders based upon their company's reputation as a great place to work and asked how they navigated the pandemic. It became obvious to me that businesses that survived and even thrived during 2020 were those that invested in their people.

Part of the investment is sponsoring benefits programs to help our employees steward their resources (like financial wellness) and programs to help them build their resources (like a workplace retirement plan). This book is a companion to my first book, *Repurposement: Experiencing the Financial Freedom to Start Living on Purpose Today.* You might say *Repurposement* is for your employees and *401(k) Architecture*[1] is for you, the employer.

I started writing this book in 2013 and set it aside to focus on *Repurposement*. But 2020 and quarantine provided an unexpected gift that helped restart the project: downtime.

As I write these words, the world is in the grips of a global pandemic. COVID-19[2] has quite literally stopped life as we know it: shuttering the economy, sheltering us in our homes, and threatening to stop the rotation of the planet. In many ways, the current situation is unprecedented. Pandemics are not new, of course, but in 2020, the connectivity reached in a global economy makes this a uniquely shared experience. Previous pandemics, albeit severe, could be isolated experiences. Even serious plagues that threatened an entire continent could be unknown by others on the planet at that time. But this virus appears to have

---

[1] In the subtitle and throughout this book, the term "401(k) plan" is used generically to describe an employer-sponsored qualified retirement plan and may just as easily refer to a 403(b) plan, a Governmental 457 plan, a 401(a) plan, or other similar arrangements, like a profit-sharing plan.

[2] This footnote is purely for historical reference. I'm not sure how future generations will come to know this period. COVID-19 is a disease caused by severe acute respiratory syndrome—coronavirus 2 (SARS-CoV-2), and even today, some will refer to "COVID-19," "Coronavirus," "SARS2," and "the virus" interchangeably. How will future generations refer to this time? Surely some in the earliest days of the Depression did not refer to it as "The Great Depression," and yet there can be no more apt term applied to that period in the 1930s.

crossed every geographic, nationalistic, and socioeconomic boundary.

In America, we have all been exposed, if not to the virus directly, to the impact of the virus. CareerBuilder found that 78% of Americans live paycheck to paycheck[3]—not 78% of lower-income workers or 78% of young workers, but 78% of *all* Americans in *all* socioeconomic strata. It is not an income issue; it is a stewardship issue. Those who make more just spend more; making more money does not create more margin. If a person is living paycheck to paycheck, missing even one or two paychecks is catastrophic. And living without margin, living beyond our means, is what the 2020 pandemic exposed for an alarmingly high number of people.

Every so often, there is a seismic shift in the world, a shifting of tectonic plates that causes a crack and then a fault and eventually an earthquake. The term "paradigm shift" is overused, because when we find ourselves in the midst of a true paradigm shift, we wish we had a stronger term for the change we're experiencing.

Sometimes the shift is only known in retrospect, but at other times, we are confident that while the impact is uncertain, we know that nothing will ever be the same again.

---

[3] As reported by *Forbes* magazine in January 2019, prior to the pandemic in 2020, so it may be even higher today.

Paradigm shifts are easily recognizable in the rearview mirror because they lead to behavior change. For example, due to the Great Depression, an entire generation of Americans handled money differently—lived, saved, and spent differently. Similarly, because of 9/11, we travel differently.

It appeared that during the Recession in 2008 we learned some valuable lessons. Americans started saving more and decreased the amount of debt that was crippling the average household. But it was not a paradigm shift, because the change in behavior was temporary. At the time, former Fed chief Alan Greenspan said that the greatest problem facing America was financial illiteracy, that far too many were living beyond their means and living on borrowed time. He said the problem had less to do with the economic downturn than the fact that the economic downturn exposed a problem: poor money habits.

So we learned better money habits and made better choices...until we did not. Until we got lazy and fell off the proverbial wagon and returned to the bondage of debt and credit. We forgot the pain, and it lost its power for change.

What will 2020 prove to be? We have all been exposed in 2020; perhaps not to the virus, but our unhealthy money habits were exposed. Far too many were living paycheck to paycheck, and a short-term interruption in revenue had immediate, catastrophic ramifications. It feels like things are different, but will the change be lasting, and will it produce good fruit? How will this impact the way we save, the way we spend, and the amount of debt we carry? How will this impact the way we work, the way we telecommute, and the way we conduct business? And how will this impact the way we live and love, the way we practice social distancing or social media distancing, and the way we interact with others?

Will we treat each other with more kindness and love? Will we become less polarized, less divided, less hateful? What choice will we make? It all starts with our choices.

I can only say, speaking from a purely economic perspective, that having *zero* debt allows us to make better choices. Having *zero* debt made a big difference in how we responded to the pandemic. There were companies and households that were strong financially and emerged even stronger, companies with "rock-solid balance sheets" and "tons of cash" that didn't just survive but actually thrived.[4]

During the quarantine, NBC News interviewed Harris Rosen of the Rosen Hotel Group in Orlando, Florida.[5] The pandemic's economic impact is still unknown at the time of this writing, but it is projected to be in the trillions of

---

[4] The Chief Economic Advisor for Allianz Investments, Mohamed El-Erian said this during an interview on CNBC during the height of the economic crisis of 2020 (El-Erian, 2020).

[5] Harris Rosen founded the Rosen Hotels & Resorts in 1974 and serves as the Orlando company's president and Chief Operating Officer. Kerry Sanders, a correspondent for NBC News, conducted the interview, which aired originally on the *NBC Nightly News*, April 1, 2020.

dollars for just the tourism industry. NBC News learned that the 5,000 employees at Rosen's eight hotels were not laid off, even after a 50% drop in business, and they asked Mr. Rosen for confirmation. He insisted that not a single person would lose their job or miss a paycheck and said that he was able to do that because his company had "no debt and a philosophy of saying we love you."

The interview Rosen gave hit both of our themes. First, Rosen's company cares—their value is love—but second, they had successful business outcomes. Rather than a choice between people or profits, investing in people was quite profitable, enough to avoid any debt.

The question is whether 2020 will be a paradigm shift, a catalyst for us to seek financial freedom after the quarantine lifts, or whether we will go back to the "normal" of living paycheck to paycheck.

Regent Bank nearly lost everything in 2008, but the lessons they learned were not about sacrificing people in favor of profits; they learned the importance of being generous, even in the face of economic challenges. Phenix Label Company faced a similar trial in 2009 but remained generous, climbed out of debt, and just completed one of their most profitable years. Because Regent Bank and Phenix Label were debt-free, both organizations survived and thrived during the COVID-19 pandemic.

The retirement plan industry was facing a crisis *before* 2020. The crisis was real, but the pain was deferred. The underfunded retirement dreams of our future are like the frog in the kettle,[6] the surrounding heat becoming gradually unbearable until it is too late to survive. Hopefully, the economic crisis of 2020 turned up the heat quickly enough to get our attention. The pandemic (the healthcare crisis) triggered falling markets, high unemployment, and a recession (the financial crisis). After hitting an all-time high on February 12, 2020, the stock market dropped more than 30% on March 23, 2020.[7]

I am writing this book from quarantine about how successful businesses navigated one of the biggest disruptions imaginable, not by choosing profits over people but by balancing their purpose and their people with their profits. Purpose-driven businesses know the secret to long-term success, and your company can benefit from the lessons of others striving to be good corporate citizens. We will start with a few inspirational stories about **why** it makes sense to invest in our people and finish with practical steps about

---

6 The boiling frog is a fable where a frog is slowly boiled to death. The premise is that a frog put suddenly into boiling water will jump out, but if the frog is put into warm water and slowly brought to a boil, it will not perceive the danger and will be cooked alive. It is a metaphor for slow reactions to dangers that arise gradually rather than suddenly. While some 19th-century experiments suggested that the underlying premise is true if the heating is extremely gradual, more recent studies have proven it false: a frog gradually heated will jump out.

7 The Dow Industrial Average closed at 29,551.42 on February 12, 2020. The S&P Index closed at 3,379.45 on February 12, 2020, but actually reached its high of 3,386.15 on February 19, 2020. By March 23, 2020, the Dow and S&P had dropped to 18,591.93 and 2,237.40—a drop of 34.85% and 30.75%, respectively.

how to design a retirement plan that serves your purpose and your people.

WHY

SECRET TO SUCCESS[1]

COMPANIES THAT BALANCE PURPOSE AND PROFITS

Successful business leaders understand the value of investing in their team, and no employee benefit makes a stronger business case for investing than financial benefits. The Consumer Financial Protection Bureau, a federal watchdog agency, estimates that employers typically see an ROI of $3 for every $1 invested in a financial well-being pro-

---

[1] In this section, I include the results of multiple interviews with successful business leaders about the ROI and VOI of taking care of their employees and investing in employee benefits. The business leaders interviewed were selected based upon workplace ratings as a top employer in their industry and may or may not be clients of PHD. Retirement Consulting. Their inclusion in this book is not an endorsement by the author of their businesses. Similarly, these interviews may not be considered an endorsement by these businesses of the author or of the advisory practice of PHD. Consulting, and as these businesses may not be clients of the author, their quotes may not be considered testimonials.

gram.[2] There is a benefit to financially healthy employees. Healthy employees stay longer, reducing the expensive cost of training and hiring replacements. They are less financially stressed and more productive when working. And they retire on time rather than working beyond their most productive years.

Companies that are regularly included on the list of top places to work have solid employee benefits as the cornerstone of employee engagement. These employers seldom have trouble recruiting or retaining top talent, and their employees often give a little bit extra because of these investments. Successful businesses garner the allegiance of a loyal workforce by communicating love in how they take care of their people.

Repeatedly, as I interviewed leaders for this book, the terms they used seemed out of place in a business context. Many of them talked about love. Many others talked about caring for their people rather than seeing employees as a means to an end. It was more than lip service because they expressed the love in dollars and cents. The correlation between successful businesses and taking care of employees was undeniable.

Coronavirus challenged the very foundation of the Rosen

---

2   From a financial wellness study conducted by the Retirement Advisor Council in collaboration with EACH Enterprise. The full report can be found online at retirementadvisor.us/report-2021.

Hotel Group, a foundation built on "a philosophy of saying we love you," a philosophy noticeably absent from most business classes.

Sean Kouplen, the president and CEO of Regent Bank, said that one of his new employees told him, "I figured out the secret at Regent Bank. The secret is love. I've never felt love before at a company. I've felt appreciated. I felt that they were glad for what we did. But not a personal love like I've experienced here."[3]

Love is hard to measure, and it is probably not something you learned in business school, but maybe it should have been. Taking care of the team is the secret to success. John Bartrom, the CEO of Jericho Home Improvements, said, "I try to stay engaged with the company...how folks are feeling, how their week's going, how their wife and kids are doing. For them to know I care is like a secret sauce that pulls us close together."[4]

The year 2020 was a test for business leaders, and the more they cared, the better they fared. It was a test of their core values, whether or not they really were at the core. Busi-

---

[3] Sean Kouplen is the Chairman and CEO of Regent Bank, as well as the Secretary of Commerce and Workforce Development for the Oklahoma Department of Commerce. The author conducted the interview with Kouplen on July 15, 2020.

[4] John Bartrom is the founder and CEO of Jericho Home Improvement, a bathroom and kitchen remodeling company. The author conducted the interview with Bartrom on March 4, 2021.

nesses that survived (or thrived) did so because they held tightly to the value of caring for the team.

Austin Hall is the Employee Experience Manager at Pro Athlete, and he acknowledges that the pandemic was a major "stress test" for his company. "There were days we were giving more money in refunds on returns than we [made] on products going out the door," he admits. "But we did not lay off or furlough anyone that's full time. One of our core values is stewardship, and we love to give back. And we [did not] want a pandemic to stop us from living up to our core values, so we were willing to pay [employees their] hourly rates to volunteer. We were able to take a hairy situation and turn it into a positive for the community."[5]

Two of the businesses I interviewed, Jericho Home Improvements and Global Prairie, were started in the heart of the Recession in 2008, and 2020 provided a test of the values upon which their companies were built. "According to the news, it was the worst time to start a business," Bartrom said. "A lot of others that I've talked to [in our industry] have really struggled. The overall market is down, but there are still some [opportunities], and those people are reaching out to us in record numbers. Sales are very strong. The struggle we have had is finding skilled labor [to keep up

---

5   Austin Hall is the Employee Experience Manager of Pro Athlete, Inc., a sporting goods retailer. The author conducted the interview with Hall on February 11, 2021.

with the demand]. We've put ads in every major city in the country. We're recruiting nationwide."

Anne St. Peter, the co-founder of Global Prairie, said, "You have to have an abundance mentality. I don't know what it is, but for me it's faith. If you have that abundance mentality, you recognize that everything unfolds for a reason…you have to believe you're on a journey, and you just have to go through it."[6] The pandemic nurtured a scarcity mentality for many people, but leaders who remained purposefully committed to decisions they had made in the beginning flourished. "If there are profits, part of those profits go to trying to make the world a better place. We throw those profits (10% of them) into our foundation, and the foundation gets distributed to causes that our team is passionate about. It was a decision that my co-founder and I had to make to be generous and not keep it," she said. "We wanted to lead in a way that was an example to our children of how we want to be remembered as business leaders. We wanted our company to be a force for good in the world."

As Kouplen put it, "You choose between the two: Am I going to maximize profits [or] am I going to love my people? The shareholder wants profits. The board wants profits. The employees want to make more money. The community wants you to give. You've got to decide who are you going to

---

[6] Anne St. Peter is a co-founder of Global Prairie, a purpose-driven global marketing firm. The author conducted the interview with St. Peter on March 12, 2021.

be. We tend to lean more on the employee side of the continuum, which makes the board unhappy at times, but that's who we're going to be, and if that's not who [the board] wants [us] to be, there are a lot of other people they can hire as CEO. That's the way I'm going to run the organization."

For perspective, both Global Prairie and Regent Bank are incredibly generous *and* incredibly profitable. "The net results are very, very good financially. We are one of the top performers in the nation," Kouplen said. And St. Peter added that their approach "outperforms typical companies in the S&P 500, anywhere from two to eight times" in spite of their generosity...or maybe because of it.

Ron Hill was the owner and Chief Enrichment Officer of Redemption Plus for 24 years. He said, "We have to care about ourselves, and we have to lead ourselves in a way that allows us to be super empathetic toward the people in our care. I genuinely think that the only way to do that is for the leaders themselves to be on a journey of growth and discovery. I believe that many people grow up with their own paradigm, their own box, their own [junk]." As Hill put it, his own "purpose journey" started after his company hit a profitability wall and he struggled to understand why. He was introduced to this concept of "purpose-driven companies," and it answered a lot of questions. Today, he is an advocate for "stakeholder capitalism, conscious capitalism, conscious leadership." He describes it as a tough lesson to learn, but once he learned how to lead himself and tap into the brilliance of others, he found success.[7]

And the success translates to ROI, sometimes measured by retention. "We have very little turnover, and I think that speaks for itself," Hall said. "Even in the entry-level positions." John Doull, the CEO of Cornerstone Bank, said, "We want to recognize that you're important to us, and we want you to feel appreciated and valued here," and then noted that the 13-year average tenure of officers at his bank is "way above average for our industry."[8]

"It's the three-legged stool," Doull said. "The employees, the clients, and the shareholders—all of them have to be taken care of, or otherwise, the stool falls over." Although he points out that there is clearly a priority to those legs on the stool. "I think employees always come first in line because if they are taken care of, they should take care of clients. My second priority is clients. Third in line is the shareholders. You put your money in, and you expect a return, but it's not the first priority. We have got to get a return for shareholders, but first, the employees need to have a safe and satisfying workplace to be a part of and to feel valued."

---

7   Ron Hill was the CEO of Redemption Plus, a product redemption business in the family entertainment industry, for 25 years. He is also a founder and Team Lead for Conscious Capitalism Kansas City. The author conducted the interview with Hill on February 26, 2021.

8   John Doull is the founder and CEO of Cornerstone Bank. The author conducted the interview with Doull on February 11, 2021.

PURPOSE-DRIVEN VALUES ARE IN THE DNA OF SOME COMPANIES

"You can't fake culture," Kouplen said. "What we hear all the time is 'This is the kindest place; people here are so nice,' but we could sure make them not nice by treating them poorly."

"There's stuff that we do that costs us money, but at the end of the day," Hall said, "taking care of people is in our DNA. There are days when I'm working hard, and it's a tough job, but if I ever thought of [leaving], I'm like, 'Holy cow, 65-year-old Austin is going to be pissed that he left this 401(k) match. Future married Austin with kids is going to regret leaving these benefits.' If you leave, you're not just losing a job and salary, but you're losing a lot of other stuff, like fringe benefits."

Hill said, "Purpose-driven means purpose as the true north and the center, so it means creating something that's larger than what you do. In a purpose-driven company, profits are balanced with purpose. We went through some really tough years of holding true to that purpose, which ultimately did create more profitability because *purpose is like a lubricant, and it reduces friction in the organization.* It aligns people."

The top three core values at Jericho Home Improvements, for example, are taking care of customers, taking care of the "Jericho family," and taking care of the "orphan and abandoned child." Bartrom said his company does a lot of things with the Global Orphan Project and is heavily involved in giving back. "It's a huge part of our culture. I think the reason we've been successful is having a heart of giving and taking care of others. Jericho is bigger than just [remodeling]. Our true calling is to take care of the orphan and abandoned child. Every employee knows that because of the work [they are] doing [they are] taking care of several children that would not have had anyone to take care of them. It's something we talk a lot about with our employees, and it's kind of our higher calling, our higher purpose, and that [is] tied in with how we treat our employees. Our employees know that they have a bigger purpose, and so they do great work. And because they do great work, more business comes."

Before St. Peter launched Global Prairie, she was "enamored with businesses that did good in the world, like Patagonia." She said, "I loved this combination of business as a force for good. I was falling in love with these purpose-oriented firms, and I decided that it would be interesting to take this Patagonia mindset and see if we could apply it to the world of consulting." The traditional approach had been a consumer product mentality—buy a product because it's going to do good for the world—but she wanted to apply that to the world of professional services. "If you would buy a product because it's good for the world, why couldn't you buy a consulting service, a law firm, a bank, an advertising agency that is doing good?"

The purpose-driven company does not happen by accident; there is intentionality involved, and circumstances often test your resolve. To pursue this avenue (and stay on course) takes tremendous effort, and some have taken the additional steps to be recognized for this work. "Certified B Corporations" (or B Corps) are businesses that meet the highest standards of verified corporate responsibility. Global Prairie, for example, is among the top 10% of all B Corps in the world. The B Corp is a rigorous certification that evaluates how a company "benefits" the world. This is a global movement most people have not yet heard of, but it is growing. Businesses are assessed on how they treat employees, how they treat the environment, and how they serve their community. "Sustainability" is an increasingly popular catchphrase, but to be recognized as a B Corp, an organization must pass the B Impact Assessment every two years to remain accredited.

Before Global Prairie, there were no global marketing firms that were B Corps. St. Peter wrote a business plan to be the first global marketing B Corp and added the objective to be 100% employee owned. They just celebrated their 13th year of successfully aligning purpose and profits, balancing "employee happiness, community engagement, and sustainability." Their business model dictates that purpose and profit be on a level playing field. And because they are employee owned, the employees are involved in those decisions. "Taking care of our employees is part of the business model, and when purpose is at the center of an enterprise, I think the alignment of [values] changes."

WHEN TAKING CARE OF EMPLOYEES IS IN THE BUSINESS MODEL

Admittedly, some of the examples below are outrageously generous and extravagant. I would encourage readers to focus on the hearts behind the benefits rather than the specifics. Some of the actions successful leaders took were not expensive—some were even free—but if they were gestures from the heart, they were impactful.

Hill had employees who would say, "'I was seen...I was heard...I shared my voice.' And these were people who worked in the warehouse and thought, 'Nobody's ever really cared about me.' Stories of people who don't speak good English, and they say at most companies the owners laughed behind [their] backs because [they] don't speak good English. At Redemption Plus, we genuinely cared. I built a family. I had a COO at one time who said, 'This is a business; this isn't a family.' Based on that conversation, I decided to double down and say, 'It's not *like* a family; it is a family. It's a work family.' Employee benefits are important, but I think even more important, ultimately, is the care. We wanted it to be an amazing place for people to come and work. We had amazing benefits. But it started with genuine care."

"It's a conscious decision you make every day to invest in your people or put money in your own pocket," Kouplen said. "It doesn't all cost money, but a lot of it does. And you just have to decide who you're going to be. When you invest in excellent benefits and make employees feel special, not only do they perform better, but they also tell their friends. There is a cost to not only the lower productivity of a low-morale employee, but there is also a cost to turnover and having to retrain."

Charles Casteel, the CFO of Phenix Label Company, said it starts with hearing and respecting your employees, neither of which costs a dime. "Letting people know not only what's going on but why. We want Phenix to be the best place that people have worked. So [we] strive to be clear about our goals and where we're going." They call it "the why with the what."[9]

It creates a culture at Phenix Label where people matter, sometimes expressed in very tangible ways. Casteel mentioned an employee who had been with the company 44 years because Phenix was flexible in accommodating her requirements with a special-needs child at home "because that's what families do." He mentioned another employee whom the entire Phenix family stepped up to care for, even though the employee had been working there for less than a month.

---

9 Charles Casteel is the CFO of Phenix Label Company. The author conducted the interview with Casteel on February 5, 2021.

"They had a house fire, and they lost everything," he said. "We sent a message out company-wide, and all the employees gathered around. Some donated couches, clothes, food. We collected money, [our owner] matched it, and we had this brand-new employee who said, 'I can't believe you did this for me' because they'd only been with us a month. But taking care of one another is what we do. One of the ways [our owner] counts himself as successful is by what he's able to give back to employees."

The benefits exceed those of most of their competitors and many big corporations because they go beyond expectations. For example, they increased payroll for coronavirus hazard pay, but Casteel said, "We recognized that the second and third shift were making some sacrifices for their family, so we doubled the differentials for those shifts. And while there's talk about a $15 minimum wage, we don't pay anybody below that. We want to make sure that people who work here don't have to have three jobs to make ends meet. We provide employees an annual statement of total rewards, and [many] comment that they had no idea we invested that much in them."

John Doull said his job description could be summarized in one word: cheerleader. "Everybody is important to me here," he said, "and we try to reiterate that just by some of the culture things we do to celebrate our staff: football contests, food days, celebrating birthdays and anniversaries, paying our employees to volunteer for our school partnership. I tell people that life is more important than the dollar and the bottom line here."

At Pro Athlete, Hall said they have 12 core values and a benefit or a perk that aligns with each one. "With our value to 'Embrace Stewardship,' for instance, we give everybody a $1,500 annual allotment to give back to any charity of their choice. You get free money to give back."

Doull admits that sometimes investing in people takes money. "We pay in the 75th percentile; we have an incentive program; we have a nice 401(k) match and pay 72% of healthcare expenses; we pay profits and bonuses; we have long- and short-term disability, and dental and vision; we give out Royals and Chiefs tickets; we do gift cards; and last year, when we received extra fees when processing the PPP loans, we shared those fees with the employees." Doull mentioned a company tradition impacted by coronavirus: the Christmas shopping spree. The event builds team morale because it is done in community, sending each employee out with $250 for Christmas shopping and asking them to be back by a certain time to show colleagues what they bought. When the pandemic altered the tradition, however, Doull said he still gave employees the money to "shop on their own schedules."

But sometimes investing in people is not expensive. Doull

mentioned their Pass the Thumbs-Up Award, where employees recognize each other. He said it was particularly impactful to receive peer affirmation. But he also noted the importance of the recognition offered from the top executive when describing a very impactful company meeting where he personally recognized everyone on the team. "I individually went through the entire staff and said some unique things about each one of them, in front of everyone, that I personally appreciated. I didn't realize how important that really was until people said afterwards that it meant so much that I recognized their unique strengths for the organization in front of the whole staff."

TAKING CARE OF PEOPLE WITH EXTRAS LIKE THEY REALLY MATTER

Kouplen said the number one thing he learned in building a successful company is that "it is all about the team. This concept of the CEO getting all the credit—a lot of times we deserve the blame, but the credit we very rarely deserve. Our culture is one in which we do tons of stuff for our employees, and I still don't know that it's enough. For example, with the Paycheck Protection Program, we took a large portion of the revenue that we made from that and paid it out in bonuses. And every time the bank grows by a $100 million in assets, we pay that number to the employees. We just hit $800 million in assets, so every employee got $800. It's [$100,000] that we could put to the bottom line, but they're the reason that we got there. And we've got a sabbatical program where, every five years, employees get an extra two weeks of vacation in addition to the regular vacation that they have to take consecutively to unplug. And we have an employee benevolence fund, and we send everyone flowers, to their home, when they start working here. And I still wonder if we're doing enough."

Part of being a B Corp is a requirement to pay employees in the 75th percentile, to offer premium benefits, to provide volunteer hours for employees, and to donate a percentage of income to charity. Global Prairie meets and exceeds these standards and actually produces better results, not by pushing employees but by encouraging them to have balance. St. Peter said the biggest challenge is getting employees to have an integrated life. "We have a very high-stress job, and the folks that we are attracting are really super high performers, people [who] push themselves. How do they unwind and relax and de-stress? If they go over 50 hours a week, I put that in red, versus in a lot of firms, where if they *don't* hit that 50-hour target, it's in red. We have a lot of young people, we recruit out of the Ivy Leagues, we recruit out of the HBCUs, and we have a lot of super bright people trying to solve social ills with leading social impact (like the person who brought Project Homeless Connect from San Francisco to Kansas City and is working with the mayor to eradicate homelessness here) while also launching new-to-market drugs for biogen in their spare time. And they're Yale grads with Stanford MBAs, and they're working 60 hours a week, and they're still volunteering, and I'm trying to tell them to slow down, giving [them] a coach [because] we really want [them] to breathe."

Bartrom said that his company pays "about 20% more than average in almost every field." He said they offer full benefits, but they also do lots of little things that add up. "Every month or so, we get together with all of our employees, like a bowling alley or a picnic. We try to break bread with our employees. We try to make sure that they feel special." Bartrom does more than just offer his employees a 401(k) match; he implores them to save enough to get the match, even though it costs him more if they invest more. He regularly tells employees, "If I went to your bank with you, and every $10 you put into your savings account, I'll pull out my wallet and put $10 in there too, how many weeks would you want me to go to your bank with you? If you must, start out at 1%, start out at 2% of your income, but do something, do a minimum of 4% because we're matching dollar for dollar up to 4%."

On the day I spoke with Ron Hill, he had just cut dozens of checks to be sent to *former* employees. His company had a "Care Fund" that employees could apply to for help because that was part of taking care of people. "I feel like if you do that, people take better care of their families, and you strengthen the fabric of society." He admits some of their benefits are unusual and some may seem paternalistic, but it is part of caring. "We [gave] people flex time so that they could integrate life and family. We had a financial wellness program from Dave Ramsey, and we had a chef on-site to provide $5 meals with no wheat, no dairy, a form of a healthier way to eat and hopefully have people not go and get the $5 taquitos at the gas station."

Pro Athlete has a chef on-site as well. "We have a lot of really cool perks and benefits," Hall said. "There's a chef, so we have free breakfast, free lunch, even snacks. That is a $10,000 perk in and of itself, spending $10 to $20 a day per employee in food, minimum. And we have a swimming pool, a sauna, a racquetball court, hair stylists on staff, pedicures, manicures, a massage therapist, a lot of really cool fringe benefits that cost substantial money, like a 10% 401(k) match and free healthcare." Hall said their commitment to keep health insurance as affordable as possible has not been easy. "But even with the rising cost after ACA we stuck to our guns, and, regardless of the hit the company is taking, employees haven't seen that fall back [on them]."

Taking care of people is not just extra benefits offset with low pay. Hall said they use an independent resource called Pay Scale to make sure compensation is within certain guidelines. "We publish [it] to the employees and say, 'Here are your ranges.' [And] if they're capped off or capped out in their position, they still get an annual cost-of-living bonus, at minimum 1.7%. The Social Security Administration marked it at 1.6% this year, but our minimum adjustment is 1.7%. Our customer service range moved up 4.17% from what it was last year."

One of the more unique benefits provided at Pro Athlete is access to free counseling. "'Create a healthy work environment' is one of our core values," Hall said. "We had a gym and racquetball court for physical wellness, we had financial wellness, but we were missing the emotional or behavioral side of wellness. [So now] we have a behavioral health therapist. Employees can make anonymous appointments to talk about whatever they want. Prior to Pro Athlete having her, I would never have gone to talk to a therapist, but I've used her, and I will continue to use her, and let me tell you what: I needed a therapist a long time ago. It's opened my eyes and helped me to spread the word [about the benefit] with some of my friends because mental health has unfortunately had such a negative connotation to it."

Hall said they offer a massage therapist and a meditation coach, and encourage employees to take time through the day, called "enrichment time" to focus on themselves. Paid time they can use to get a haircut, to work out, to meditate, or whatever they need. It's all part of how they say, "People matter here."

Bartrom agrees that there is a return on investing in your

people. "We had an employee who got some kind of rare infection," he said. "It had nothing to do with work, but he was in the hospital like three weeks, and he couldn't afford to take three weeks unpaid as an hourly employee. I told our VP of Operations that we're going to pay him hourly until he's back. The VP was worried that if we do that for one person, we have to do that for everyone, but I [didn't] care. We were going to do it for this guy, and we will consider it on a case-by-case basis. I doubt if all our employees are put in the hospital for weeks. I went and visited this guy in the hospital and prayed with him and told him what we were going to do, and he starts crying, amazed that we would do this for him. It's things like that that touch an employee's heart that cause folks to say they're going to stay with this company forever. And our employees do stay. What's more important than truly giving back or taking care of our employees and making sure that they're loved? What I've experienced in my life is that when you do those things, everything else figures itself out."

Unfortunately, taking care of employees is not always the norm, and taking care of former employees is even rarer. But Bartrom talked favorably of former employees, even helping them transition out if that was the next step in their career. And Hall talked about Pro Athlete's "Hall of Fame" for former employees. "We call it the 'legends of the hall,' where we induct past employees—anybody who's helped us [get] to where we are today. [Our owner] takes very little recognition of himself. He started the Hall of Fame to recognize all the folks that helped the company get to where it is. Any employee who was here for at least a year and left on good terms is in the Hall."

Far too many employers take departures personally. When a former employer like the New England Patriots congratulates Tom Brady on winning another Super Bowl (in a Tampa Bay Buccaneers jersey), it is rare. But it should not be rare. Successful business leaders understand the value of taking care of people, and an extension of taking care of them is wishing them the best...and if their best is somewhere else, helping them to get there.

Treating people the same, whether they are still on the team or on to the next team, shows congruence in our care.

When employees feel the love and care, it produces better results. Providing just a little something extra nets a little more effort. "The more fulfilled [employees] feel," Bartrom said, "the better they take care of the customer, the more efficient they are, and the less turnover we have." It is a direct return on investment.

"It is all designed to let an employee know how much we value them," Kouplen said. "And [it] builds energy for the organization. I believe very strongly that an organization needs energy. There is a level that they can work to do the minimum, and you may not know it, but then there is this additional effort and creativity and innovation that they can do above that, and that gap is what we are trying to capture with all that we do."

And what a leader does is so much more impactful than what they say. Kouplen referenced his dual role as both the CEO of the bank and the State Secretary of Commerce for Oklahoma. "At the state, I have 36 different agencies [requiring] more time over there. I am still giving the rah-rah speeches as the cheerleader at the bank; I am still in the employee meeting to say, 'great job,' 'new record.' I am still sending emails. I am still saying all the right stuff. But it is 100% what you do. As John Maxwell teaches, congruence is the most powerful business skill in the world. When people know that you are the same all the time, and you are not going to treat them one way here and then a different way in a different setting, like 'I love you as long as you work for me, but when you walk out the door, I slander you and treat you poorly,' or 'I love you when you are doing great, and then I treat you bad whenever you make a mistake.' If people see that lack of congruence, it creates a lot of issues within an organization. I have to be the same all the time regardless of circumstances."

On the day I spoke with Secretary Kouplen, he had just learned Tesla would not be building a new facility in Tulsa after months of courting this opportunity for economic growth in the state. "We found out last night that [Tesla] is not coming to Tulsa. I had two options, and I am going to respond in kindness to them when this goes public [the harder of the two options]. You want to be frustrated, but we must be consistent. I am at peace with it, confident that everything is going to work out and confident that we left everything on the field. We did everything we could do."

Kouplen understands that congruence is just as important in his next hire at the bank as it is in the next deal for the state.

WHAT ABOUT THOSE WHO DON'T CARE? WHO DON'T SEE THE ROI?

Anne St. Peter said, "It's a better business model [to balance people and purpose and profits]. I was doing it to make my business stronger, but it was making me happier and making me a better human to engage in the community. It was like a win-win-win."

Austin Hall said, "It's kind of a hybrid between ROI and VOI. Our CEO wrote a blog post titled 'It Doesn't Cost...It Pays.'" At Pro Athlete, they believe there is a quantifiable return on the investment.

Charles Casteel said, "It's just the right thing to do, to take care of your people. But you also do the right thing because it returns happier, healthier, more content employees who will go the extra mile when you need them to. Happier employees *will* return in dollars and cents beyond the immediate payoff in morale. Retention is huge. And as compared to the manufacturing industry, we're well ahead of the average. Our accounting manager is one example. A single mom without a high school diploma, they taught her what she needed to know, and she worked hard and worked her way up to a leadership role with us. And the supervisor in our warehouse area was a press operator when he started." Long tenures are a huge return on investment.

Ron Hill added, "I don't think doing it the way we have always done it will be sustainable, because I think people will start to vote with their dollars. If you do not take care of your employees, if you do not care, it will eventually cost you more." Hill believes the ROI is clear; it just depends on how you measure it. "We tracked turnover and longevity. Overall, we were trying to reduce waste and rework and increase the efficiency so we could give that money back in terms of compensation. We never just paid minimum wage. We always paid what was a living wage, and then we added the benefits on top of that. The [ROI] was the cost [of] turnover. The more you can reduce, there is a huge return on those benefits. But I think when you throw benefits at people without creating a foundation of care, then I don't think that there is as much return on it."

Hall said Pro Athlete also measures ROI in retention. "We have very little turnover," he said, "even in the entry-level positions. The person who wants my job may have to grow up and out (to advance their career), but that is about our only turnover. People stay once they are hired because they know we care. And I can speak to that firsthand. I had a sister who was going through chemo, and every other Friday when she had her treatments, I went to sit with her. I worked four-day workweeks for almost one year, at the support of everybody in the company. One of our core values is 'family first,' and I have experienced it."

Cornerstone Bank sees the return on investment (and the cost of not investing) from a different perspective—from the perspective of their commercial clients. "We have a thousand clients who are business owners," Doull said. "Most business owners have realized the power of the employee is pretty great in their business, but the failures in our loan cases primarily occur because of poor management decisions. You cannot overcome poor management. It's greed; it's pride; it's obstinance; but if there's no humility, that business owner's not really willing to learn and listen. [During the pandemic] most of our businesses had some pivoting they had to do, and I think part of that is to listen... to your spouse, to your employees. Making the almighty dollar doesn't matter when you're in the casket. You cannot take it with you, so care for your people."

St. Peter discussed making it through the pandemic, not by cutting costs but by investing more in her people. "We probably had 15 'enterprise value projects' going to keep the team busy. We did not lay off. We said to them, 'We are going to be loyal to you; we need you to stay busy.' We had an enormously positive reaction because they saw that we were taking care of them. We looked at our brand; we looked at our website; we looked at products that we wanted to create. Last year, if you look at the publicly traded comparables, their stock price decreased, and our stock price was a double-digit increase."

It pays to take care of employees, yet some business owners are still unconvinced. They do not believe that there is an ROI to taking care of the team (or a cost of not doing so). "I think the only way to reach that type of an individual who just doesn't really care," Kouplen said, "is to show them that it is a win for them. And it is. I mean, we have grown 40% a year for 10 years in a row, in an industry that averages 3%. And the only magic is taking care of our people. It benefits you, as a business owner, to do this. It is not completely altruistic. Growing up in a home where my dad was a farmer and my mom was a bank teller—and neither one of them liked their jobs and griped all the time about their jobs—I want our people to go home in the evenings and talk good about their jobs. I think it impacts their kids and their marriage. That was my number one objective: to create a place where people would feel good when they went home at night. The net results, however, are great financially. We were just named the seventh top lender in the nation."

"I don't know how you change a person's heart, and I don't know how you quantify that number," Casteel said, "but I believe that number exists [on the ROI]. I think that even if it did not, we would still do it, but I also think that it is there. And it shows up in less absenteeism, low turnover. Happy employees are good employees. They pay attention to what they are doing. Not having to work [multiple] jobs allows [them] to be more alert. And when you are given authority to make decisions—like *Should I stop the press because this isn't good enough quality?*—it translates into better and higher morale. It is a mutual respect, and it is mutually beneficial. Phenix is profitable, and even in those challenging years, we continued to give out a monetary Christmas gift, even when we lost money. We were generous, even when times were bad. And if times are good, how much more money do we need to make? As Gordon Gekko said in the movie *Wall Street*, 'How many boats can you ski behind?' We have people who leave, and almost immediately they want to come back because they realized not every company cares."

Getting companies to care starts with transformational leadership, which starts with leaders being transformed. Bartrom said, "Share your heart and be open with your people. If they can see your heart, that can create transformation." But first the leader's heart must change. Ron Hill said he started his company because of his own experience in the workplace, where he felt like "how long my butt sat in that seat all day was way more important than who I was as an individual. I wanted to run a business differently but kept getting this pushback, like 'When you're really successful, then you can take care of people.' But my internal compass was telling me the whole time that I could do both."

THE LEADER AT THE TOP MUST BE THE CHIEF CARING OFFICER

Having proved that it is possible (and profitable) to both care for people and successfully grow the bottom line, other business leaders sought the advice of Ron Hill to transform their companies. But a caring culture must begin with the Chief Caring Officer.

"I've had friends who run companies that said they believe in the whole conscious capitalism piece and asked me, 'So who's the best person in my organization to go make this happen?' And the answer is never what they want. I tell them, 'It is you. You have to go on a journey.' Where I think the most impact gets to be made is in building leaders of tomorrow because I think people of a certain age either get it or it is like 'I am where I am.'" In other words, they are not willing to go on the journey and be transformed themselves.

Casteel agrees that it starts with the "lead servant" and referenced a podcast from Patrick Lencioni. "[Lencioni] said one of the things he can't stand is this term 'servant leadership.' It all should be servant leadership. And adding 'servant' makes it seem like it's possible to have leadership without the servant piece."

Leadership is tested by whether the executives act in the best interest of their people. Do they care about what is best for each employee? Doull said, "I want you to be a better banker, even if you leave me to go somewhere else. I want to have contributed to your success in learning something about our industry and making you more valuable to whoever you work for next."

This is a rare response, which is why the New England Patriots' post congratulating Tom Brady stood out. Many do not celebrate those who have moved on and moved up. "The person who wants my job," Hall said, "may have to grow up and out [to advance their career], and that's perfectly fine. I had a former employee of ours, he was an entry-level warehouse worker for us but, after a while, became overqualified in his position. He knew he needed to do more for his family, for both personal growth and professional growth, so he left to be a warehouse manager at another company, but he still stays in touch. His new boss said, 'I have never had an employee still in communication with their former job. I think that is really cool.'"

Hall went on to say, "I could have a conversation with [our owners] and say, 'Here's where I am in my career; here's where I want to be; I'm thinking about going here or there,' and they would say, 'How do I help you get there?' Meanwhile, a friend of mine who works at another company was looking around, and his company found his résumé online and nearly terminated him! He wants to better himself, which might mean he goes somewhere else on good terms, and he almost lost his job because management was like, 'Whoa, you're looking for another job? Shame on you!' That is not the way it should work...but that is typical."

Purpose-driven companies are purposeful about helping employees find their purpose or, if their purpose does not lie within that organization, helping them to grow up and out to a place that aligns with their purpose.

"I love the idea of 'repurposement' rather than retirement," Hill said. "The idea of helping people find their purpose and tying that to the company purpose. My idea of retirement was my grandfather, who wore a jumpsuit and sat in his chair and watched TV and chewed on cigars, and then he died. So that is my impression of retirement, and I do not want that. People say to me now, since selling my company, 'How is it to be retired?' and I have to say, 'I sold my business, but I am not retired.' I am passionate about my own purpose and how to make an impact in the world, so I love that idea of *Repurposement*."

Conscious leadership requires taking care of our employees, which starts with benefits that serve our purpose and our people. We do it because there is a clear and measurable ROI. But we also do it because it is just the right thing to do. If you are a business leader, you are a steward of your company and your employees and their families and beneficiaries, and sound stewardship produces successful business outcomes as well as successful retirement outcomes.

401(K) AS THE CORNERSTONE

THE EASIEST, MOST PROFITABLE WAY TO CARE FOR THE TEAM

In the previous chapter, I shared stories of highly successful businesses noted for taking care of their employees. Perhaps it was inspiring, or perhaps it was daunting. But rest assured, it is not necessary that you hire a chef, put in a racquetball court, install a swimming pool, or pay for 100% of your team's health insurance. In fact, the easiest and most effective employee benefit—the foundational piece in taking care of your employees—is perhaps the most affordable and profitable: the company retirement plan. Having a 401(k) that works is the cornerstone; it's the one piece to the benefits package you have to get right, and yet so many employers get it wrong.

In this chapter, I will discuss why some plans do not work as well and the keys to making your retirement plan work. And I will continue to explore the ROI with 401(k) plans. Having a workplace retirement plan that works is not that expensive, though having one that does not work might be terribly expensive.

At the writing of these words, hundreds of thousands of Americans have lost their lives to COVID,[1] an unspeakable tragedy by any measure, but many will also die this year in America from heart disease, cancer, stroke, hospital-acquired infections, and the common flu.[2]

Why, then, did the pandemic fester so much fear, produce so much anxiety and hoarding, and lead to so much scarcity? (There was actually a run on...toilet paper!) According to the American Institute of Stress, 120,000 people die

---

1 As of January 14, 2021, there have been more than 92 million confirmed cases worldwide with nearly 2 million deaths, and more than 23 million cases in the US with more than 386,000 deaths, according to the Johns Hopkins University Coronavirus Resource Center (Center for Systems Science and Engineering, 2021).

2 According to the Centers for Disease Control and Prevention (CDC), there are approximately 17 million deaths worldwide—647,000 Americans—from heart disease each year. They estimate 1.7 million hospital-associated infections, from all types of bacteria, that contribute approximately 100,000 deaths, and as many as 56,000 people die from the flu or flu-like illnesses in an average year. The American Cancer Society projects 1,806,590 new cases and 606,520 deaths this year alone. And according to the Stroke Center, more than 140,000 people die each year from stroke in the United States. Stroke is the leading cause of serious long-term disability in our country. Each year, approximately 795,000 people suffer a stroke.

every year as a direct result of work-related stress, suggesting anxiety induced by the virus could cause as many deaths as the virus. Why are deaths unrelated to the virus not receiving as much attention?

Part of the explanation for the panic is the spotlight on COVID-19. (If the evening news kept a daily tally of the number of hospital-acquired infections and deaths, none of us would visit the doctor.) But most of the explanation is the sensationalism caused by so many dying simultaneously. It gets our attention because it is out of the ordinary. Every day, 3,287 Americans die in car accidents,[3] but unless a bunch of them die in the same accident, it does not make the news. It is not rational when we consider the statistics, but most of us fear flying much more than driving.

Unhealthy retirement plans that produce unhealthy retirement outcomes—broken retirement plans that are killing our retirement dreams—are like auto accidents, claiming many more victims but only one at a time. A precipitous drop in the market that impacts all of us simultaneously gets our attention, but without the stock market crash of 2020, the average American's retirement plan account was already underfunded, and many would have been "pushed" into retirement this year (due to their age) without the

---

3   Nearly 1.25 million people are killed in car accidents each year, more than heart disease and cancer combined. That means, on average, auto accidents cause 3,287 deaths per day. An additional 20 to 50 million people are injured or disabled, according to AAA.

financial means to actually retire (apart from acquiring a second job in retirement).

This book is about how to build healthy retirement plans that actually work, and the stakes are high for getting this right because the cost of failure is even higher. So *why* isn't this getting more attention? Because it is not a plane crash. Cars (and flus) kill many people but not all at once, which allows us to tolerate those realities, even accepting them as normal.

Broke has become the new normal—mountains of debt are normal; underfunded retirement accounts are normal—but it does not have to be.

If the impact of COVID-19 was significant enough to cause a paradigm shift, maybe we will have a new normal.

WHY THE TYPICAL 401(K) PLAN DOES *NOT* WORK

The employer-sponsored retirement plan works better than anything else as a means of building wealth and preparing for the future (this is *not* a case *against* participating in the company 401k plan), but it does not work as well as it could or should. And there are a variety of reasons for those failures. The biggest three are:

1. The fees are *still* too high

2. Most plans are poorly designed
3. Few plans receive the appropriate expertise

If you think of other reasons they fail, send me your suggestions, and we might include them in future editions of this book.

A big reason is that **the fees are *still* too high**. I emphasize "still" because there has been a tremendous amount of fee compression in the industry in the last few years, but, in many cases, the employees are still overpaying for their plan. A deeper discussion of plan fees is covered in Chapter 8, but, in brief, the cost issue can be summarized by poor comparisons, burdensome regulations, and outdated service models.

The typical investment held in an Individual Retirement Account (IRA) is more expensive than the typical investment held in a 401(k) plan. It is simply the law of large numbers. There are breakpoints and pricing considerations for larger institutional accounts. The typical advisory fee in an IRA is 1% or more, while the typical advisory fee in a 401(k) plan is half that amount or less.

If the typical investment fees and advisory fees are much higher in an IRA, it stands to reason that the 401(k) plan is much cheaper, even after adding the cost for recordkeeping and administration. In reality, it is generally cheaper but not as cheap as it should be.

Some plans are still using the more expensive retail share class of funds rather than institutional or retirement share classes. And with fee compression, some financial professionals found additional revenue sources, like adding proprietary funds or portfolios, or adding expensive Managed Accounts programs.

Regulators also exacerbate the issue with burdensome reporting and service requirements. While there is greater complexity (and cost) servicing large institutional accounts, in theory, the costs should be spread over more people to reduce expenses. The problem is that regulators sometimes create too great a burden to spread.

In the spirit of protecting plan participants, for example, the requirement for increased notification continues to grow, and these are costs that the service providers pass on to those same plan participants. Only very recently, legislators *finally* allowed electronic notifications; previously, regulators required mountains of paperwork to be mailed to every employee's home, notifications that were almost certainly not read by anyone. It was wasteful at best but unnecessarily burdensome (and expensive) at worst.

An example of outdated service models would be service providers that did not adjust to incorporate electronic delivery or did not adjust pricing after electronic notifications were permitted. Many service providers had the cost of printing and shipping notices baked in, and when regulators lifted this burden, they pocketed the extra margin as additional profit. Service models reliant upon dated technology are less profitable and therefore more expensive to plan participants.

Another reason some plans do not work is that **most plans are poorly designed.** Plan design is complicated. It requires a deep understanding of the guidelines under the Employee Retirement Income Security Act of 1974, as amended (ERISA), enhanced by a basic understanding of behavioral science (and how employees might respond to nuances in those plan designs). Unfortunately, plan design is almost exclusively the responsibility and burden of the employer sponsoring the plan. The overall authority to manage and control the operations and administration of the retirement plan is held by the Plan Administrator—not a TPA, or third-party administrator, but *the* Plan Administrator (capital "P," capital "A")—and, by default, this is almost always the employer. The employer can outsource *some* of the fiduciary responsibility to third-party fiduciaries (as we will discuss in Chapter 5), but the employer is always ultimately *the* fiduciary. An employer who sponsors a qualified retirement plan can never *not* be a fiduciary.

The problem with relegating something as important as plan design to the employer is the lack of that employer's experience and expertise in plan design. The employer's experience is in building widgets or providing services in their industry, and their only experience with plan design is with the design of their own plan. Complicating matters further, plan design is considered a "settlor function" under ERISA, and settlor functions are not eligible to be paid from plan assets.[4] Most service providers, including fiduciary advisers, *are* paid from plan assets. So while most service providers, including fiduciary advisors, are more experienced than the employers they serve in matters of plan design, they are prohibited from offering that expertise or are required to do so without compensation. Regulations have cut off employers from their best source of advice about plan design.

As a result, **few plans receive the needed expertise** to be successful. The employers (aka the plan fiduciaries) are seldom served by plan fiduciary advisors. In fact, less than 5% of retirement plans are even served by professional retirement plan advisors, fiduciary advisors dedicated to the retirement plan industry, despite research that suggests an overwhelming benefit of working with a financial professional who specializes in this area. In a study conducted by research group EACH Enterprise, LLC, Plan Sponsors were surveyed about successful retirement plan outcomes, and those results were compared

---

4   Settlor functions include decisions about whether or not to create or terminate a plan, or whether or not to amend the design of an existing plan, or determining who the plan will cover, or designing the benefit offerings and plan design features.

to whether the plan received guidance or expertise from a third-party advisor. Of the employers that participated in the research, 18.2% worked with no advisor, 20.4% worked with an advisor "doing some work with retirement plans," 38.3% worked with an advisor "working primarily with retirement plans," and 23.1% worked with an advisor "working exclusively with retirement plans." The study found better results for employers working with an advisor than without an advisor, and even better results for employers working with a specialist. Contributions were higher, more employees were on track to retire, and more employers found the plan easier to administer when partnering with an advisor, and even more so when partnering with a dedicated advisor who "worked exclusively with retirement plans."

Ironically, while the retirement plans themselves are heavily regulated, the advisors serving those plans are much less regulated. Services are rendered by insurance agents who specialize in annuities, wealth managers who specialize in high-net-worth accounts, or individual financial advisors who specialize in personal insurance. Seldom are services rendered by dedicated specialists who work exclusively with retirement plans. In fact, no additional certification or licensing is even required to serve a 401(k) plan, leaving most plans without the expertise needed to be successful because the employers have not hired an expert with the experience needed.

WHAT DOES A SUCCESSFUL (HEALTHY) PLAN LOOK LIKE?

One of the issues during the pandemic was identifying confirmed cases of COVID-19. Some test kits were unreliable, producing "false negative" results. Compounding the confusion, some had the disease with few or no symptoms.

A healthy response to the pandemic required that more people be tested and more people be tested more accurately.

A healthy response to the retirement plan crisis requires that more plans be tested and more plans be tested more accurately.

We miss the obvious signs of an unhealthy or broken plan because we use the wrong test. The only test that matters is whether the plan actually helps people retire better. What is the plan's retirement rate? In evaluating a college, for instance, it is appropriate to judge effectiveness by looking at the graduation rate. (I realize some measure success on the gridiron rather than in the classroom, but the graduation rate matters.)

Many retirement plans do *not* help plan participants retire better, and yet this alarmingly high failure rate is missed because the test is broken. The three Fs of Funds, Fees, and Fiduciary is no longer the standard. After all, a retirement plan with really good funds is still a failure if too few employees are investing in those investments. And a plan with really low fees is a failure if it still produces really low results. And a plan that reduces fiduciary liability is a failure if too few employees retire well (because unpreparedness creates its own liability).

"Funds, Fees, and Fiduciary" falls short. The alliteration helped it stick, and salespeople made it part of their schtick, selling us a solution that appealed to our greed (funds and fees) or fears (fiduciary liability), with little regard for the "F factor" that makes the biggest impact.

The fourth F is Fruit, as in, "What kind of fruit does the plan bear?" It is really the only test that matters. "Every good tree bears good fruit, but a bad tree bears bad fruit. A good tree cannot bear bad fruit, and a bad tree cannot bear good fruit...Thus, by their fruit you will recognize them."[5] Quite literally, a healthy plan should naturally produce healthy retirement outcomes.

This is not to say funds, fees, and fiduciary are unimportant, but their importance is secondary to the fruit the plan bears because the goal is to help as many people as possible get across the finish line.

Only 51% of private industry workers have access to a

---

5   Matthew 7.17-18, 20 NIV

company retirement plan,[6] which is why the SECURE Act, passed in 2019, was created: to close the retirement gap. Fifty-one percent is a failing grade.

Of those workplaces that offer a retirement plan, the average participation rate is 84.9%,[7] a passing grade but not a fantastic grade.

And the average savings rate among those who are participating is only 6.8%,[8] about half of what is recommended. The contribution rates are limited by the IRS, but only 13% of plan participants max out their contributions and hit the limit.[9] And savings rates at 50% of what they should be is a failing grade.

The result is an average account balance (before 2020) of $100,000.[10] While most Americans have less than $10,000 saved for retirement,[11] even $100,000 is unlikely to be enough for most of us.

---

6 According to the US Bureau of Labor Statistics, 51% of workers have access to only a Defined Contribution plan; 13% have access to both a Defined Contribution plan and a Defined Benefit pension plan.

7 As of January 2019, according to the American Benefits Council.

8 As of 2018, according to Vanguard 401(k) data, as reported by US News & World Report.

9 US News & World Report, 2018.

10 Fidelity Investments announced that average 401(k) balances had reached record highs at the end of 2019—$112,300, compared to $105,200 at the end of September 2019 and $95,600 the year before—but estimates are that these were negatively impacted by the pandemic.

11 Fifty-two percent have less than $10,000 saved for retirement, according to a *USA Today* poll (Hellmich, 2014).

A successful (healthy) plan is one that has enough people saving enough money so everyone retires on time (and retires with dignity). A plan that works does not leave anyone behind.

And yet we accept mediocre results as the norm. Perhaps you know your employees are saving too little, but you are at a loss for how to correct this. Perhaps you wish for better results, but you take a rising balance as an indication that things are okay. Just okay is not okay, and rising markets with new contributions can hide plans that are not okay. From June of 2009 until the financial crisis in 2020, the US economy experienced 129 consecutive months of positive GDP growth, the *longest* expansion in the US economy *ever*...in the entire history of our country. We had an 11-year bull market (when the average bull market is about 2.75 years long), so everyone's plan looked okay. Unfortunately, rising markets mask a lot of mistakes. Bolstered by adding new money each payroll cycle, even mediocre returns and incompetent advisors look okay; when new contributions are constantly being made, of course the account balance rises, particularly in a good market. The question is, How much healthier might those balances be if even more employees had saved more money, if the fund performance was even better, or if the fees were more reasonable?

Might there have been no one left behind? Might there have

been even more people retiring on time and retiring with dignity?

THE VALUE (AND BENEFIT) OF PLAN HEALTH

As we learned with COVID-19, some who are unhealthy may not exhibit symptoms and, *if* asymptomatic, may wonder, *What's the harm?* The implication is that many plans do not work or do not work as well as they could, but is there a cost to being unhealthy?

There is obviously a benefit for *employees* to retire well, but there is also a benefit to the *employer* if employees retire on time, a benefit that directly impacts your bottom line. Beyond altruistic reasons for promoting plan health, there are financial reasons.

An aging workforce still employed beyond their most productive years will cost you in lost productivity and absenteeism, higher insurance premiums, and higher wages. Longer tenured workers simply cost more.

According to one survey, as workers age, they are less able to work and/or more limited in their ability to work.[12] The increased absenteeism may be due to disability claims, as older employees are more likely to file for workers' comp

---

12 According to a National Health Survey conducted by Sloan Institute in 2005, 19.1% of workers age 65 to 69, as compared to 13.3% of workers age 45 to 64.

and have longer workers' comp claims, more expensive benefit payments, and higher medical bills. This is due to the severity of the injury and the increased number of treatments needed.

And if an aging workforce is financially stressed about their inability to retire, their financial troubles can decrease productivity in the workplace by as much as 20 hours per month.[13]

And it should come as no surprise that older employees are more expensive to insure. Your insurance premiums increase drastically with the age of your employees, both your healthcare premiums and your disability insurance. If employees are not financially well enough to retire, your premiums pay the price.

Workers' comp costs will depend on the industry—any industry with a higher potential for injury runs an even greater risk of increased injuries the longer employees stay past normal retirement age—but every industry is subject to some increases for an aging population.

Insurance is expensive, but underinsured workers are not the solution. According to a Gallup Poll, 30% of workers

---

[13] According to Smart Dollar and Ramsey Solutions.

have put off medical treatment because of the cost in the last 12 months, which only exacerbates the issues.[14]

And, of course, beyond the cost of insurance and benefits, the biggest expense is payroll. The mature employee with decades of experience is probably paid more than younger employees.

A recent Financial Finesse case study reports that employees cost an additional $10,000 to $50,000 per year for every year they delay retirement beyond normal retirement age.

I am not suggesting we force employees into retirement prematurely, but a worthy goal of a retirement plan is helping them retire with dignity on their own terms. If an employee does not want to keep working, I hope they have the financial means to retire. After all, if you still have "retirees" working who do not want to be there, it is not great for morale or productivity.

Perhaps you wish to invest in a healthy retirement plan for your employees, but you have wondered if it is worth the investment.

"What's the ROI?"

---

14 Gallup Poll, 2014.

It is a fair question, and the answer can be quantified in dollars and cents. It does not have to be quantitative versus qualitative—ROI versus VOI[15]—because healthy retirement plans make sense for both the employee and the employer. In fact, you may not be able to afford to *not* have a healthy retirement plan.

Understanding that there is an ROI and why healthy plans are critical is the first step to maximizing the 401(k).

---

15 Return on investment versus the value of investment.

3

REPURPOSEMENT

UNDERSTANDING WHY WE BUILD HEALTHY 401(K) PLANS

Parents are inundated with "whys" from their kids. It is tiring, particularly when "whys" devolve to "why-ning." Sometimes we wish for blind obedience, but obedience comes easier when we understand the why. In fact, understanding the why nets the same result even if no one is looking.

During the pandemic, some officials called for mandates on wearing masks to keep the virus from spreading, but other officials understood that education would get a better long-term response. Mandates may produce short-term results, but understanding why is crucial to ongoing benefits and long-term advantages. We need to know the why in order to comply.

Retirement is a long-term goal—a marathon—and successfully running the race requires understanding why.

In my previous book, I advocated for replacing "retirement" with "repurposement." Rather than a singular date on the calendar (historically at age 65), I propose a transitional journey toward purpose and then repurpose and ultimately repurposement. After all, in the traditional framing of retirement, employees "graduate" from something (work) to...what? Repurposement is about reframing the transition around purpose, which starts with having the end in mind and understanding why.

It is important to start building wealth by knowing our why. Why embark on this journey? Why is it worth the sacrifice and time and energy? Studies have shown that employees who look at a picture of their family right before electing their contribution rate select a higher savings rate because they remind themselves why (and for whom) they save. Other studies have shown higher investment rates among employees who look at an age-progressed picture of themselves to call to mind what might be at stake.[1]

In this chapter, we unpack why employees should remain committed over time and why you should invest in benefits

---

1 *Repurposement*, p. 27, Lexington, KY, Mahout Press Inc., 2019. (ISBN 978-1-7340927-0-7) (https://www.amazon.com/Repurposement-Experiencing-Financial-Freedom-Purpose/dp/ 173409270X/ref=sr_1_1?dchild=1&keywords=repurposement&qid=1587656677&sr=8-1)

for your employees. To remain purpose-driven, the prize must be clear.

Knowing why is key, as is having the right why, a goal worthy of our long-term commitment. In *Repurposement*, I hypothesize that the root of the retirement problem in America may be that we aim for the wrong objective. As we were reminded during quarantine, passing the day bingeing on Netflix gets old fast. It is meaningless. And retirees who pass the day watching television until they pass may wish they had passed a bit longer on stepping into retirement.

I think there is a better path, a purpose-driven path. Rather than *working like a dog*, I would advocate for *finding your purpose*. And rather than *retirement*, I would advocate for *repurposement*. And rather than *rest*, I would rather pursue a *calling*...After all, rather than just settling for *death*, our heart's desire is to aim for *legacy*, leaving something to this world greater than ourselves.

If the Typical Path is a descension—from Working to Retiring to Resting to Death; a Better Path might be an ascension—from Purpose to Repurposement to Calling to Legacy.[2]

Employees need to understand why it is important to get in (and stay in) the healthy plans we build, or they will be

---

2 *Repurposement*, 2019, pp. 38-39.

tempted to make an early exit and sabotage their future.[3] And you need to understand why it is worth the investment to not take shortcuts in building the plan.

Repurposement requires understanding the big picture: the flight path, destination, and fuel necessary to make the journey.

And investing in repurposement requires understanding the ROI.

Knowing why (for you and your employees) is key to success.

THE FLIGHT PATH FOR A HEALTHY RETIREMENT PLAN

Most people like to know the destination before embarking on a journey. Others insist on seeing the roadmap. A clarification of the path keeps passengers from straying off course. I use the "Flight Path for a Healthy Retirement Plan" to explain the process.

---

[3] A great way to provide this understanding for every employee is to put a copy of *Repurposement* in the hand of your entire workforce. We wanted to reward readers of this book (and diligent readers of the footnotes in this book) with a special offer. Email me directly (troy@PHDfirm.com) and mention where you read about this special offer to provide a bulk rate when ordering books for every employee on payroll. We will ship the books to you at our cost of printing and shipping—zero profit margin—no tricks and no obligation required. It can be an employee group of any size, as long as you are ordering a book for every employee. Twelve employees or 12,000 employees, we will provide the book at cost.

The idea of a retirement plan taking the path of a "retirement *plane*" is not a new concept, and variations of this illustration have been used by others in the industry for years. Specifically, the idea of a "retirement plane" is discussed by Shlomo Benartzi, cocreator with Richard Thaler of the acclaimed Save More Tomorrow™ program. Benartzi references three phases centered upon the role of automation in plan design: to fly, fly higher, and fly smoother—to Save, Save More, and Save Smarter—he encourages auto-enrollment, auto-escalation, and auto-diversification, respectively. In fact, those who use auto-enrollment will experience "auto-takeoff" rather than being "auto-grounded." And those using auto-escalation experience an "auto-climb" rather than an "auto-hold." And those properly diversified should experience a ride described as "auto-smooth" rather than "auto-turbulent."[4]

Benartzi's "Retirement Plane" is similar to the first three phases in my flight path, though we discuss the entire journey from start to finish—not just taking off but landing the plane as well.

The first step in the journey is simply getting on the plane. I call it "Takeoff" because the plane *will* take off, with or without us. I can recall flying in the not-too-distant past when gate agents would hold a plane for connecting flights that were delayed, but that rarely happens today with the

---

[4] *Save More Tomorrow*, Shlomo Benartzi, pp. 27–29, Penguin Publishing, 2012.

emphasis of on-time departures. Similarly, the flight to retirement is also on a tight schedule, driven by our age or mandated by age if the company has mandatory retirement.[5] The planes are not sitting on the runway until we are ready because the passengers are not getting younger.

Employees must understand the importance of getting on the plane and starting the journey as soon as possible. Thanks to the power of compounding interest, those initial deposits matter even if they are small deposits. Employees must understand why this is critical for success, whether motivated by greed to build a huge nest egg or by the fear of diminishing support from Social Security; whatever inspires them, they must be compelled to get on board. It is hard to imagine a scenario where it does not make sense to participate in the workplace retirement plan, so participation should (in theory) be 100%.

You can't afford to save? Just do 1%, but do something.

Doing nothing—saving 0%—is a certain way to fail the test. And, yes, there will be a test at the end. It is called retirement. And while it is possible to delay retirement a bit, it cannot be delayed forever.

---

5 As a result of the Age Discrimination in Employment Act (ADEA), there is no mandatory age for retirement. In other words, an employer cannot generally force an employee to retire, except when they can. In rare cases, there is still mandatory retirement. An example of this happens with air traffic controllers, who are required to retire by age 56. In other industries, the requirement is less overt, though the cultural dynamics might still marginalize aging employees and effectively produce the same result.

Unfortunately, doing nothing is exactly how many employees respond to this monumental decision. Whether the inaction is rooted in procrastination or ignorance, many *employees take no action at all*. This makes it particularly important to make sure the defaults for the retirement plan are set up to help and not harm the goal of getting every employee across the finish line. Every plan has a default: a default is simply what happens when *employees take no action at all*. In other words, the default is what happens in the absence of a specific election. Every employee is given the opportunity to make an election, but if an employee does nothing, what happens? Are they in the plan, or do they have to specifically elect to be in the plan (an "opt-in" election)? The default setting should be to have everyone in the plan unless they specifically elect to not be in the plan (an "opt-out" election).

Everyone has an option, of course. No employee is forced to participate. An employee can choose to opt out. But if they do nothing, we want to make sure the plane does not take off without them.

The assumption is that everyone wants to retire someday and that anyone left behind will regret missing the flight. The default should put them on the plane, nudging them toward a destination they desire (a nudge for which they should thank us later).

We also must understand why it is so important to "Climb." There are reasons to climb in retirement, just as there are reasons a plane climbs in flight: climbing is key to success.

Planes climb above the clouds (over 30,000 feet) so they can fly faster. The higher the altitude, the thinner the air, and the less resistance in the atmosphere, the more efficient the flight. It is also safer for cruising at a higher altitude because birds are no longer a threat.[6]

Retirement accounts also need to climb to be efficient. Some passengers get on board at a low entry point (like 1%), but a successful journey requires more fuel. In fact, successful outcomes require a lot more than most are willing to pay. We recommend a contribution rate of 15% (just for the employee contributions). And very few employees can go from 0% to 15% at the start.

It is also true that few employees go from their initial rate to their target rate on their own—without a nudge or two along the way. Again, this is where defaults can help or hurt. A default of auto-increasing employees facilitates success. Without auto-increase, the default is to leave employees at their initial election. Without help to climb, most will

---

[6] "Here's How High Planes Actually Fly, According to Experts," by Celine Hacobian, Time Magazine, June 27, 2018. https://time.com/5309905/how-high-do-planes-fly/#:~:text=Commercial%20aircraft%20typically%20fly%20between,a%20flight%2C%20according%20to%20Beckman.&text=And%20the%20weight%20of%20the%20plane%20changes%20as,climbs%20higher%20into%20the%20sky

not. The gravitational pull is simply too great; there are too many demands for our money. Investing another dollar toward the future will only happen by design and effort and sacrifice.

Planes will generally reach their cruising altitude within the first 10 minutes. Similarly, retirement accounts should reach cruising altitude within the first 10 years. A reasonable starting point, on average, is 5% to 6% with increases of 1% a year to 15%. Those who start lower or start later may need annual increases of 2% to get on track quicker. The point is, the sooner the account is at 15% or more, the better the chance of long-term success.

We also need to understand why it is important, upon reaching "Cruise" to simply put it on cruise control and leave it alone. I call it IDNO (pronounced "Ida know"). It's an acronym for the "Importance of Doing NOthing" because passengers who sit back and let the professionals fly the plane arrive safely, while those who try to take control midflight may not.

Elsewhere in this book and in *Repurposement*, I discuss the common mistakes of market timing and self-directing, and how micromanaging the retirement plan spells disaster. Those who do not understand this touch their accounts too much—to their detriment. It is critical that everyone understands why *not* touching the account is important.

Just telling them not to touch it almost guarantees they will touch it! People need to know the why in order to comply.

In 2020, because of the pandemic, the stock market dropped sharply between February 12 and March 23. In fact, it was a drop of almost 35%. The best thing to have done when the roller coaster plunged was hang on; the worst thing to have done was jump off midflight.

One of the participants we work with made a very costly mistake because they did not understand why. As the market dropped, they became nervous. They watched it dropping through mid-March, and, finally, on March 18, they pulled the plug and moved to cash to prevent further losses. As the market continued dropping on the 19th and 20th, they felt like they had dodged a bullet. On March 23, when the stock market bottomed out, they were sitting safely on the sidelines. And they sat out of the market even as it recovered through April. Finally, in May, they decided to get back into the market. Because the market had rebounded, most quarterly statements were positive, some showing double-digit returns. But this participant, who had moved to cash, had a significant loss.

It was not a comfortable conversation, explaining *again* that we encourage employees to *not* touch their account. If this employee had remained in the same portfolio throughout the year, their second quarter statement would have shown a 12% increase. Instead, the statement showed a 7% decrease, a loss of 19% from where the portfolio could have been if it had been untouched. Selling low (in March) and buying high (in May) cost the employee 19%, a $190,000 loss on a million-dollar account. That is an expensive lesson learned about market timing!

Cruise control does not prevent turbulence, but, hopefully, when turbulence strikes, leaving the account on cruise control keeps us from making a mistake. Putting it on cruise control means setting it to a glidepath (a professionally managed portfolio that is properly diversified) and leaving it alone.

A few decades later, as we near our destination, we prepare to land, a concept discussed in depth in my previous book. In fact, the last chapter of *Repurposement* is devoted entirely to helping passengers find a harbor pilot to safely complete the journey.

"Preparing to Land" includes setting goals, fine-tuning budgets, and identifying the right pilot to land safely. Most of the journey is completed with automated features, but landing is not done on autopilot. To safely land, we need a specialist (a Certified Financial Planner, CFP®) just as the flight required a specialist (a Certified Plan Fiduciary Advisor, CPFA®).

Having the right pilot is the difference between success and disaster in the final step: "Land." There is so much attention on the accumulation phase of retirement and too little attention on the distribution phase. The only solution the financial industry provided historically was a guaranteed annuity. With the best of intentions, the financial industry tried to apply the pension model to the 401(k). Some embraced the concept because their greatest fear was outliving their money. But some financial advisors took advantage of their fears to sell expensive products that reduced their savings.

In a pension plan, participants receive a Defined Benefit—a fixed amount per month—and the employer has a growing liability to pay the benefits. Shifting from Defined Benefit to Defined Contribution shifted the liability from the employer to the employee. The shift benefited you, of course, but it also benefited your employees in allowing unlimited benefits. In the pension model, the benefits were capped (defined), but in the 401(k) model, the benefits were limitless (theoretically)—defined by how much each employee saved.

One of our clients had employees retiring extremely well after only modest salaries because the employer (a Fortune 500 company) enrolled every employee in the plan and provided a nice company match with company stock. Those who stayed in the plan and stayed with the company for many decades were literally retiring as millionaires after years on the assembly line. They retired more comfortably than they would ever have retired under the old pension model.

With an annuity, 401(k) participants buy the benefit of the Defined Benefit model (levelized payments) in exchange for surrendering the benefit of the Defined Contribution model (uncapped revenue). Settling for an annuity can be an expensive mistake, as annuities erode years of hard labor with excessive fees.

Landing is hard. In fact, it is the most dangerous part of flying. A successful flight can be wrecked by landing in a storm (a chaotic market). I have piloted a small plane, and I can say from personal experience that landing was the scariest part of the experience. Descending is dangerous because this is where the birds fly (read: the vultures), but landing is even more dangerous. Hitting a bird is super inconvenient, but hitting the ground is even less convenient: the first is expensive, but the second is catastrophic. Landing successfully requires a pro.

THE FUEL NECESSARY FOR A SUCCESSFUL FLIGHT

Effective retirement education centers upon one idea: anything beyond the message of "save more" is peripheral, confusing clutter and possibly harmful.

Traditional retirement education failed to move the needle on successful outcomes. It focused on investing, as if more investment knowledge produces better results. The objective of traditional retirement education is helping plan participants make sound investment choices, and yet every study suggests they should not be making their own investment choices.

The goal of retirement education should not be producing a room full of Chief Investment Officers; the goal should be producing a room full of Chief Savings Officers.

If a person fails to put enough fuel in the tank, they will not get their retirement vehicle across the finish line. They will run out of gas. And retirement education that covers anything beyond this point is unnecessary.

The American Society of Pension Professionals & Actuaries (ASPPA)[7] found the least important driver of retirement success is the actual investment, what ASPPA termed the "asset quality." In other words, when choosing a particular investment (like which large-cap growth fund to offer in the plan), the decision has very little impact on long-term success: it is only 2% of the factor.

According to ASPPA, the diversification of the investments

---

7   The American Society of Pension Professionals & Actuaries (ASPPA) is an organization of actuaries, consultants, administrators, and other benefits professionals.

(what ASPPA termed the "asset allocation") is 10 times more important. In other words, it is less important which investment fund is chosen and more important how much is allocated toward each particular fund.

In terms of the "drivers of retirement success," the choice of which investment funds to offer and how to diversify investments within those funds is only 22% of the equation: the "asset quality" is 2% and the "asset allocation" is 20%. The most important driver of retirement success is the contribution rate.

Ironically, the same study found that the factors that were least important, like picking funds, received the most time and attention, while measures to increase contribution rates got the least attention.

More recently, the Empower Institute conducted independent research to test these theories, with very similar conclusions. They examined four drivers of retirement wealth accumulation to identify "What matters most": fund selection, asset allocation, account rebalancing, or deferral rates?

Asset allocation was important. (Aggressive portfolios outperformed conservative portfolios.) But increasing deferral rates was much more important. The baseline return of a conservative portfolio with 3% contributions was $205,551.

Doubling the risk from conservative to aggressive produced a return that increased from $205,551 to $333,345 (an increase of 62.17%), while increasing the savings rate from 3% to 6% increased it to $411,101 (an increase of 100%). The savings rate makes the biggest impact.

The purpose of retirement education must emphasize that how much we save matters. Understanding the impact of saving just 1% more outweighs any number of lessons about investing.

THE ROI AND VOI: UNDERSTANDING WHY HEALTHY PLANS MATTER

Understanding why helps employees stay on course, but knowing why also helps you, as the employer, build the course. Building a 401(k) plan that works is not cheap. It requires an investment of time, energy, and money. And some employers may wonder if it is worth it. The ROI (return on investment) describes the money a business makes compared to the associated cost. The VOI (value of investment) is a more holistic measure to evaluate workplace culture and employee wellness. A 401(k) can and should be measured by both metrics.

I believe there is a tremendous ROI, but it is not worth investing in the 401(k) at all...if the 401(k) is not healthy, if it is not producing healthy outcomes, and if it does not work.

A broken 401(k) does not help to attract or retain employees, it still costs time and money to administer, and it increases liability for the company.

If the plan is broken, if it is not producing desirable outcomes, and if there is no plan to fix the plan, it probably is *not* worth it.

Take it out back and put it down.

But many successful businesses were built with the understanding that human resources are the most valuable resource—that taking care of your people is job number one—and providing employee benefits is key to taking care of employees. A fully functioning 401(k) is foundational in this process.

I will spend the remaining chapters explaining how to design a fully functioning 401(k) that serves your purpose and your people.

TAKING OFF...

The Flight Path for a Healthy Retirement Plan

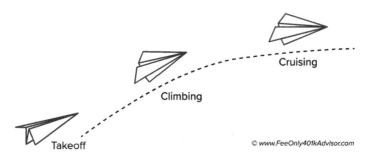

Takeoff—What are the defaults for the retirement plan, and are they set to help or harm the objective of getting every employee across the finish line? We would hate for the plane to take off with anyone left behind.

Climbing—The participants in a retirement plan do not just automatically climb toward their retirement goals unless there is an intentional and purposeful effort to facilitate the process. If fees are excessive, if contributions are low, or if the communication and guidance in the breakroom is not on target, the gravitational pull will prevent success.

Cruising—The participants in a retirement plan have the opportunity to set the flight to cruise control once they reach their cruising altitude, meaning proper diversification and rebalancing of their account along a customized glidepath. Using cruise control should mean less turbulence over the course of the journey and should promote better long-term success.

...LANDING

The Flight Path for a Healthy Retirement Plan

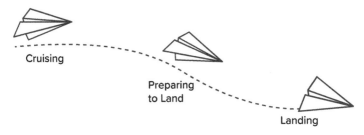

> **Preparing to Land**—The closer an employee gets to the end of their journey, the greater the importance of customized personal guidance. Have they considered where they would like to land, when they can land, and how much fuel they need to land? Have they factored into the equation Social Security and ongoing healthcare costs? It is important to sit down with a coach for in-depth planning, a trusted planner who embodies a teacher's heart and a servant mindset. Finding the right pilot is key.
>
> **Landing**—There is so much attention on the accumulation process toward retirement and too little focus on the distribution process. How an employee lands is critical. A safe landing is vital to success, and there is nothing automatic about the process. A successful landing means avoiding coming down in a dangerous spot, like a down market or a runway littered with annuities that can erode years of hard work with excessive fees. Landing the plane may be the most dangerous part of flying and must be left to the professionals.

HOW

DESIGNING HEALTHY PLANS

THE FIRST THING TO DO WHEN BUILDING A PLAN

Imagine, if you will, a successful football team that does not define roles and expectations and does not establish a leader. It is hard to imagine because it defies reality. Even the most spontaneous of backyard games has a degree of infrastructure. Perhaps the pickup game kids play lacks tryouts and formal positions, but the reason they huddle is to decide who does what. And as teams grow progressively more organized, they have the opportunity for increasingly more success. The same holds true for the company retirement plan.

The first thing to do when building a plan is to have a plan—to establish roles and responsibilities as well as establishing who is in charge. In this chapter, I outline the "cast of characters" we need for a healthy retirement plan. But the first step in designing a successful plan is forming the Retirement Plan Committee (RPC).

The first step in establishing a healthy retirement plan is often missed—by the employers, by other service providers, and sometimes even by legal counsel. In other words, a qualified retirement plan *can* operate without this step, but it is not advisable. Sometimes, upon engagement to provide advisory services, we must build or rebuild the RPC.

Legally speaking, a plan is not established until the plan document is in place (and the IRS approval letter is granted). But the RPC should be established first to decide the plan design in setting up the plan document and to govern the process. Plan governance starts with this committee.

Drafting the plan document requires decisions, as does the initial decision to acquire an IRS determination letter or the eventual decision to hire service providers. Before you do anything else, establish the RPC authorized to make these decisions.

When a company sponsors a workplace retirement plan, the company is a plan fiduciary—in a corporate sense—but implicit within this corporate designation are the actual individual decision makers who carry personal fiduciary liability. Regardless of what industry the corporation was previously in, the company is now in the fiduciary business. The prudent thing to do is identify who the plan fiduciaries are—the individuals entrusted with responsibility.

Amazingly, many companies miss this crucial first step. Decisions were made by someone, of course, but without a prudent process in place—without the legal structure of a formal committee—that person stands alone, without any mitigation of risk. Our first step in consulting with a new client is often forming the RPC. We were engaged with a large law firm, and our first order of business was drafting the board resolution to establish the committee to hire our firm. The plan had been in place for 43 years and held more than $43 million but had no formal committee.

WHY DO SOME EMPLOYERS *NOT* HAVE A COMMITTEE?

Sometimes, when starting, the formal structure of a committee seems unnecessary, and later, as it grows, it seems to be working okay without this formality. There is no "de minimis" provision under ERISA, however, meaning a retirement plan is never too trivial or minor to merit serious legal consideration. In fact, a Plan Sponsor is equally liable for a workplace retirement plan of $1 million as they are for a plan of $10 million or $100 million. I recommend putting the RPC in place before a single dollar hits the account. You are not protected by a "de minimis safe harbor" if your company or company retirement plan is small.

Or sometimes an organization's excuse is that they have a board of directors assuming some of the functions of the RPC, though the board meets less frequently, and the retirement plan is seldom on the crowded agenda when they meet. This was the case for the aforementioned law firm. The board retained the legal authority but lacked the structure or consistency to effectively manage due diligence. A large university retirement plan with which we were engaged was in a similar scenario. The board of trustees for the entire multicampus university met annually, and one of the breakout committees (the Finance Committee) was responsible for all financial matters, including the budget, endowment, and all employee benefits. And tucked deep inside the agenda for the board that only met once a year was the oversight of a $50 million retirement plan. It was an afterthought.

Or sometimes the responsibility falls on the owner, president, or CFO, without anyone to share the fiduciary burden.

The employer is a plan fiduciary, and someone is either the named fiduciary or functional fiduciary, with personal liability. Naming the RPC is part of documenting a defensible due diligence process to mitigate liability for the employer and each member of the committee.

You may have noticed I refer to it as the "Retirement Plan Committee" rather than "Investment Committee." This is more than just semantics. An Investment Committee focuses on investments. A Retirement Plan Committee focuses on the entire business of sponsoring a retirement plan: the fiduciary process, fiduciary training, and fiduciary calendar; measurements of plan health, like participation and savings; participant education; financial wellness; plan fees and benchmarking the costs; the fiduciary responsibility of monitoring and benchmarking vendors and service providers; and, finally, the fiduciary responsibility of monitoring investments. A healthy 401(k) plan should have more than *just* an Investment Committee.

HOW TO BUILD A RETIREMENT PLAN COMMITTEE

In the previous section, I referenced the unsavory proposition of having the liability fall on one person without the support of a RPC. But the size of the committee is not the issue. What is important are *structure*, *formality*, *process*, and *documentation*. A single decision maker, meeting regularly and consistently with a plan advisor and documenting the process, constitutes a legitimate RPC.

Below are some guidelines for establishing the RPC. These

are not legal or regulatory requirements but best practices based on decades of experience.

STRUCTURE—THE MEMBERSHIP OF THE COMMITTEE

A committee should be large enough to be representative but small enough to be effective. Committee members are tasked with making decisions on behalf of the entire workforce, so it may be appropriate to have departments represented. At the same time, if the committee is too large, it may be difficult to manage. And the larger the committee, the more common the absenteeism. Ongoing discussions are challenging if members of a larger committee are inconsistent in their attendance.

A committee may consist of ownership and management as well as employees of the organization. Due to the personal liability, the committee should not invite observers or non-fiduciary members, including service providers and vendors. Each person represented in the meeting should be a fiduciary. This may include an advisor, if the advisor assumes a fiduciary role.

Typically, no individual serves as a permanent member of the committee, though certain positions may hold an ex officio place on the committee, such as the CFO or Human Resources.

Identify the makeup of a committee that uniquely fits each culture. Best practices suggest an uneven number of members to break a tie in discussions or voting, for example, but in some company cultures, there are no ties to be broken, particularly if the boss is in the room. In other cultures, every department must be represented. Hopefully, the number of departments is small enough to keep the committee from becoming unwieldy.

FORMALITY—THE PURPOSE AND AUTHORITY OF THE COMMITTEE

The committee should have a charter that outlines the purpose and responsibility, defines membership, and establishes guidelines.

The committee has general responsibility for oversight of those factors and practices that contribute toward plan success and successful participant outcomes, including regular monitoring of the investment options within the plan, the participation rate of the employees in the company, and the savings rate of those participating. The committee also has general responsibilities that are administrative and noninvestment related.

The charter should indicate whether the RPC is designated as a "named fiduciary" (the Plan Administrator) within the meaning of ERISA 402(a)2. And the charter should define the personal fiduciary liability of each member of the committee as well as any efforts taken to mitigate fiduciary liability, including procedures for meeting and keeping records of the meetings.

The charter itemizes the responsibilities of the committee and describes the authority to fulfill these functions. Typical committee tasks might include selecting, supervising, monitoring, and replacing the investments within the plan; establishing and periodically reviewing the policy statements for the plan; ensuring appropriate diversification of plan investments and monitoring plan costs; appointing, monitoring, and replacing the Investment Managers and service providers of the plan; appointing other fiduciaries or service providers for the plan; administering the plan in keeping with the plan document and appropriate regulations; adopting amendments that change plan design; and enacting those measures that facilitate greater participation and savings, with an effort to enhance participant outcomes.

The charter may seem unnecessary, but it is important to establish the legitimacy and authority for a committee tasked with a very serious legal responsibility.

PROCESS—THE FREQUENCY AND MEANS BY WHICH TO MEET

The charter should also define how often the RPC meets,

what constitutes a quorum when meeting, and whether virtual participation and electronic voting are allowed.

The RPC should meet quarterly but must not meet less than annually. A quarterly rhythm falls within "best practices" because investment returns are reported on a quarterly basis. Under no circumstance should the RPC meet less often than annually. In fact, while it may not be a violation of ERISA, it is certainly imprudent for the employer, and an advisor could be out of compliance if collecting advisory fees and not facilitating an annual review.

The charter should define the required quorum, in person or virtual, to conduct business. A large committee may have a requirement for a minimum number of in-person attendees, allowing for the others to join virtually and still meet the quorum.

Speaking of size, the amount of assets should not determine the frequency of meetings; the amount of *work* should determine the frequency of meetings. The RPC of a small 401(k) plan does not have less responsibility to meet; again, there is no de minimis rule. But neither is there a mandate for larger plans to meet more often, unless the complexities create more work. Regardless of size, frequent meetings may be needed to get a program on track, but once the plan is in a healthy place, the RPC can meet less often.

DOCUMENTATION—MAINTAINING RECORDS OF COMMITTEE MEETINGS

ERISA is all about document, document, document.

From a regulatory perspective, if there are not minutes of a meeting, the meeting never happened. Each committee should create, maintain, and store accurate records, documenting the due diligence process to protect the plan, the plan's participants, the employer, the committee, and each member of the committee.

Best practices for documentation include minutes to record attendance, discussion items, decisions rendered, and action items; signing the minutes in approval; and storing executed copies of the minutes in perpetuity.

The minutes should convey a concise record of the proceedings without quoting committee members. Keep in mind that the minutes become part of the permanent record and are subject to subpoena, although maintaining no records creates more liability. The goal is to be able to demonstrate procedural prudence in the event of an audit, so maintaining records is important.

THE CAST OF CHARACTERS

In the next several chapters, I elaborate on the roles of each party, but the main cast of characters involves the following:

- **Plan Sponsor**—Employer sponsoring the retirement plan.
- **Retirement Plan Committee**—Always the Primary Fiduciary, generally consisting of some employees from the Plan Sponsor as well as the plan advisor. May fill the role of the Plan Administrator and plan trustee, or the trustee could be an individual on the RPC. The RPC has the ability to outsource some (but not all) fiduciary liability if using an ERISA 3(21), ERISA 3(38), or ERISA 3(16) Fiduciary.
- **ERISA**—The Employee Retirement Income Security Act of 1974, as amended. The governing body of law for all employee benefit plans (retirement/pension as well as healthcare), the fiduciary aspects of which are enforced by the US Department of Labor (DOL).
- **Plan Advisor**—Serves in a fiduciary role if serving an ERISA plan, in either an ERISA 3(21) or ERISA 3(38) capacity.
- **Recordkeeper**—The service provider who keeps records, sponsors the website that stores those records, and sends statements to plan participants. Generally, the Recordkeeper is not serving in a fiduciary capacity but a directed capacity (directed by one of the plan fiduciaries).
- **Custodian**—Not a fiduciary and not among the main cast of characters, as they are generally not engaged by the Plan Sponsor but by the Recordkeeper to custody assets.

- **Administrator**—The Recordkeeper can be the Administrator or may outsource administrative responsibilities to an outside or third-party administrator (TPA). The Administrator is typically not a fiduciary and fulfills settlor functions and clerical duties, such as plan testing and regulatory filing, but may serve in a fiduciary role if serving as an ERISA 3(16) Administrative Fiduciary.

In the next chapter, I outline the fiduciary roles, then the role of the plan advisor, and then the Recordkeeper/Administrator. But the first step in designing a successful plan is to have the RPC in place.

If you skipped this step, back up and form the committee to start documenting the process before designing or building your 401(k) plan.

5

MITIGATING RISK

UNDERSTANDING (AND OUTSOURCING) FIDUCIARY LIABILITY

Perhaps you heard of fiduciary liability, but you dismissed it (hoping it did not apply to you) or diminished it (banking on a de minimis exception for a smaller plan). The concept of outsourcing fiduciary liability sounded like buying flood insurance when you do not reside in a floodplain.

But when you sponsor a workplace retirement plan, you immediately become a fiduciary—the highest legal duty of one party to another—and the valley where your company resides becomes a floodplain. The fiduciary is bound ethically and legally to always act in the best interest of the other party. Sponsoring a retirement plan involves an incredible amount of risk and liability.

Practically speaking, here is what the situation looks like. Imagine you sponsor a 401(k) plan for a company of 100 employees. Your company may not have a conference room big enough to hold everyone, and even if it did, you would not want everyone involved in plan decisions (like which Recordkeeper to hire, which investments to offer, or whether to allow loans). But someone (hopefully the RPC) must make these decisions on behalf of the other employees. The decisions impact the financial future of every employee in your company and must reflect what is solely in the best interest of the employees (even if it is not what is best for the company). A fiduciary makes the decisions on behalf of the others and owes every employee the duties of good faith and trust.

Before designing and building the retirement plan, it is prudent (and legally required) to secure bonding and insurance.

The Plan Sponsor—serving as Plan Administrator and named fiduciary—is *always* a fiduciary for the plan and can never completely avoid fiduciary responsibility. At the risk of being repetitive, I am reemphasizing this point because some employers are misled to believe they can shed the fiduciary role by hiring third-party fiduciaries. This claim is misleading and inaccurate, and the persons making the claim are acting in willful deception or ignorance. One financial advisor told employers that by hiring their firm as an ERISA 3(38) Fiduciary they hire a "Primary Fiduciary"—a misleading statement because the implication is that the employer is no longer the Primary Fiduciary by having hired a 3(38).

The only way an employer gets out of the fiduciary business is to stop sponsoring a workplace retirement plan. You cannot eliminate all fiduciary liability, but you can mitigate *some* liability.

HOW TO DECREASE (MITIGATE AND OUTSOURCE) FIDUCIARY LIABILITY

It mitigates risk to be properly insured and bonded, to maintain a well-documented due diligence process, to follow the guidance of well-crafted policy statements, and to outsource responsibilities to a third-party fiduciary. Each step reduces some liability.

There are three different types of insurance policies, for example. An ERISA fidelity bond is a type of insurance policy that protects the plan against a loss caused by acts of fraud or dishonesty. This policy is listed first because it is coverage required for every 401(k) plan. It protects the plan (and plan participants) from the employer (and, in effect, protects the company as well). The DOL defines fraudulent or dishonest acts committed against the workplace retirement plan to include theft, embezzlement, misappropriation, forgery, larceny, or similar actions. The guilty parties would face criminal prosecution, and any losses would be returned to the plan by the ERISA fidelity bond on behalf of plan participants.

Fiduciary liability insurance is not the same as an ERISA bond. The bond protects the plan (and plan participants); the liability insurance protects the plan fiduciaries and, in some cases, the plan. Fiduciary liability insurance is a good idea, a best practice, but is not legally required. It protects the fiduciaries from losses caused by a breach of fiduciary responsibility. Having this type of coverage does not satisfy a fidelity bond required by ERISA, but since it is relatively easy and inexpensive to obtain, many companies add it.

A third, albeit similar, policy is Directors and Officers (D&O) liability insurance. It protects the personal assets of directors and officers in the event that they are personally sued by employees, vendors, competitors, investors, customers, or other parties for actual or alleged wrongful acts in managing a company. The management decisions covered are beyond those of the retirement plan but do also cover decisions related to the workplace retirement plan. It also is not required, but companies may add this rider to their general liability insurance policy.

In addition to having proper insurance, it also mitigates risk to maintain a well-documented due diligence process—a plan for your plan. As mentioned previously, the key with ERISA is documentation. Maintaining good records helps mitigate risk, protecting the plan and the company that sponsors the plan.

Every plan should maintain (and update) some version of a basic due diligence file. We call our process the Health & Wellness System since our focus is on maintaining healthy retirement plans to produce healthy retirement outcomes. It is necessary to have some version of a documentable and defensible due diligence process. It is also necessary to maintain good records, easily retrievable in the event of an audit. Some records may be maintained in hard copy, but most records can be maintained electronically. A fiduciary vault accessed by the fiduciary advisor and Plan Sponsor, with provisional access granted to auditors, is ideal if online security can be ensured.

The Health & Wellness System we customize for each client includes the basic due diligence files: policy statements, minutes, investment reviews, review of plan fees, administrative reports, education materials, employee notifications, and plan documents. In addition, our Health & Wellness System also includes a fee disclosure report, fiduciary training, a log of employee meetings, the behavioral audit, the glidepath optimization analysis, tracks participation and savings, and outlines the fiduciary roles.

Implementing policy statements—if done correctly—also mitigates risk and reduces some fiduciary liability. The policy statements are maintained in the due diligence file. The reason for having this as a separate step is to highlight the importance of these policies and clarify some common misunderstandings.

The most common policy statement is the Investment Policy Statement (IPS). Many plans have an IPS, but despite its ubiquitous nature, it is not required. Having an IPS is considered a best practice. The irony is that, while not required, regulations imply that it should be, and, while not mandated, regulators often ask for a copy of the IPS during an audit.

Many plans have adopted an IPS, though some plans do not have a very good IPS. It is good to have an IPS. It is bad not to have an IPS. But it is worse to have an IPS and not follow it.

While an IPS is not specifically required under ERISA, you are responsible for monitoring plan investments, and the IPS sets the standard by which the funds are evaluated. An IPS helps the RPC...until it does not help the committee.

Best practices for an IPS include guardrails that help but do not hinder. An IPS that is too restrictive places the plan and the committee at risk of being out of compliance. For example, the committee may desire investments with top quartile performance but would be wise to write an IPS that only *requires* funds to be in the top half of their benchmark. This does not prevent the RPC from still managing to top quartile standards—funds could be in the top decile, exceeding expectations—but it keeps the RPC from being in violation of the IPS if funds fall outside the top quartile. In other words, the policy statements must be crafted to protect and not punish, to serve as guardrails and not handcuffs. Policy statements that are too strict draw lines that are difficult to remain within and exacerbate liability when lines are crossed.

Best practices for an IPS also require that the policy statement be regularly reviewed and approved. In fact, this might be written in the IPS. If the RPC never reviews the IPS, funds are not monitored to this standard, the IPS may be outdated, and the RPC may be in violation of its own policy by not regularly reviewing the policy.

The fiduciary duty to monitor funds is generally understood, but less known is the fiduciary duty to educate plan participants. The duty to educate is facilitated by a good Education Policy Statement (EPS), outlining the means and schedule for providing guidance, the type of advice allowed, and the tools for facilitating healthy retirement outcomes.

And there is also a fiduciary duty to monitor plan expenses

and to properly disclose fees and performance to plan participants. This responsibility is fulfilled with a Disclosure Policy Statement (DPS) that includes benchmarking for comparative purposes.

Good policy statements, crafted with appropriate flexibility and reviewed regularly, help the Retirement Plan Committee.

A fourth means of mitigating fiduciary liability is outsourcing responsibilities to a third-party fiduciary. I mention this provision last because this is the step most employers jump to and the only step some employers take, ignoring the incredible value of the first three steps. Yes, it is prudent to outsource as much fiduciary responsibility as possible, but it would be imprudent not to also be properly insured, maintain appropriate documentation, and implement sound policies to guide decision-making. For example, it makes sense to hire a third-party fiduciary, but the decision to hire the outside fiduciary is, in itself, a fiduciary decision and must be properly documented. Maintaining appropriate documentation of a thorough due diligence process is always important, and it serves as a precursor to additional steps taken to reduce liability.

What *can* be mitigated and what *should* be outsourced? It is not possible to outsource *all* fiduciary liability—the primary role of the fiduciary will always be held by the Plan Sponsor—but it is possible for you to outsource many of the responsibilities to "subfiduciaries" to mitigate a piece of the overall liability puzzle.

I am not an ERISA attorney, and this is not intended to be a legal definition of the various fiduciary roles under ERISA. I am a plan fiduciary advisor,[1] and in such capacity, I advise plan fiduciaries, providing guidance to help employers understand ERISA without all the legalese. What follows is a nonlegal layman's guide to understanding the differences between the types of fiduciaries.

The foundation of outsourcing fiduciary responsibility is based upon the "Prudent Man Rule"[2] to act with the prudence of a person familiar with such matters and rooted in ERISA Section 404(a)(1), which says that when a fiduciary is not familiar with such matters, they are to "discharge their duties" to those who are familiar.[3]

---

1   I am actually a Certified Plan Fiduciary Advisor (CPFA®), a specific designation granted by the National Association of Plan Advisors as part of the American Retirement Association.

2   The Prudent Man Rule is based on common law stemming from an 1830 Massachusetts court ruling. It directs trustees "to observe how men of prudence, discretion and intelligence manage their own affairs, not in regard to speculation, but in regard to the permanent disposition of their funds, considering the probable income, as well as the probable safety of the capital to be invested."

3   Under ERISA Section 404(a)(1), a fiduciary is to discharge their duties regarding a plan solely in the interest of the participants and beneficiaries and for the exclusive purpose of providing benefits to participants and their beneficiaries; and defraying reasonable expenses of administering the plan. A fiduciary is to do so "with the care, skill, prudence and diligence under the circumstances then prevailing that a prudent man acting in a like capacity and familiar with such matters would use in the conduct of an enterprise of a like character and with like aims; by diversifying the investments of the plan so as to minimize the risk of large losses, unless under the circumstances it is clearly prudent not to do so; and in accordance with the documents and instruments governing the plan insofar as such documents and instruments are consistent with the provisions of other sections of ERISA."

If a person were building a house, for instance, it would not be prudent for them to personally take up construction of the building...unless, of course, construction is their business. Similarly, if a person is building a 401(k) plan, it would not be prudent for them to build it themselves unless they are familiar with such matters: plan design, fund management, fiduciary duties, and the behavioral dynamics of employee benefit plans.

If 401(k) management is not their profession and not part of their core competencies, ERISA charges them with the responsibility to discharge these duties, duties like administration and investment management, and the third-party fiduciary is only liable for their portion of responsibility.

At the top of the fiduciary hierarchy is the employer, the "named fiduciary" under ERISA 402(a), although a person can become a fiduciary by holding certain positions in administration of the plan to perform one or more of the functions described in ERISA 3(21)(A). In other words, there are named fiduciaries and functional fiduciaries.

The employer is also the Plan Administrator under ERISA 3(16) unless the employer engages an ERISA 3(16) Administrative Fiduciary. A TPA is *not* a fiduciary unless they specifically assume in writing the fiduciary responsibilities for administration. And the Administrator is not a true 3(16) Fiduciary unless they have authority to sign and execute administrative reports and filings, like Form 5500.[4] If the TPA assumes fiduciary responsibility in writing, functions as a fiduciary with administration, and signs Form 5500, the TPA is a 3(16) Administrative Fiduciary. Hence, administrative responsibilities are one of the fiduciary responsibilities the employer may discharge.

Another duty you may discharge is investment responsibility. The question is whether you want to discharge all the investment responsibility—including discretion for investment decisions. This will determine whether it is appropriate to discharge those duties to a 3(21) Fiduciary or a 3(38) Fiduciary.

An ERISA 3(21) Fiduciary is sometimes called a "Co-Fiduciary" or "Investment Advisor." They serve as a Co-Fiduciary with the Retirement Plan Committee, sharing fiduciary liability between an employer and advisor provided in ERISA 405(a), relating to the general rules of Co-Fiduciary responsibility. And they serve as an Investment Fiduciary in recommending plan investments. The key is that a 3(21) Fiduciary advises the employer, but the employer makes the final decision.

---

4   This is often misunderstood and/or misrepresented. A TPA may assume responsibility for administration, but not legal or fiduciary responsibility, under ERISA 3(16), meaning the TPA is not legally responsible for whether the administration is correct; they are acting under the direction of the Plan Administrator (the employer) who retains all the legal responsibility under 3(16). Confusing the issue further, some Recordkeepers or TPAs will claim to be a 3(16) Fiduciary, but they will not sign the Form 5500 filing, meaning that they are a limited-scope 3(16) Fiduciary at best.

An ERISA 3(38) fiduciary is called an "Investment Fiduciary" or "Investment Manager." The 3(38) advisor is responsible for the investment selection, monitoring, and replacement of investment options. The biggest difference between a 3(21) and a 3(38) Fiduciary is discretion; a 3(21) advises the employer but does not manage assets, while a 3(38) takes discretion and manages plan assets, including managing custom portfolios or Managed Accounts.

Both fiduciary roles are important, and neither role is superior to the other. At issue is how much control and discretion you want to surrender for investments. But even in selecting a 3(38), you only outsource responsibility for funds, not responsibility for the plan. You are still ultimately responsible.

ERISA Sections 402 and 405 govern the outsourcing of fiduciary responsibility and make it clear that while it is possible (and prudent) to outsource certain duties, you may not outsource the responsibility of monitoring the fiduciaries to whom you outsourced particular duties. You have the burden of due diligence in selecting the fiduciary and maintain an ongoing obligation to review the performance of each fiduciary.

Every employer (who sponsors a plan) is a plan fiduciary and should hire a plan fiduciary advisor, either a 3(21) or 3(38) advisor.

In combination with the first three steps, it is prudent for you to hire a 3(16) Administrative Fiduciary and a 3(21) Co-Fiduciary and (if wishing to surrender discretion and add managed portfolios) a 3(38) Investment Manager. These four steps together can mitigate some of the risk in sponsoring a workplace retirement plan.

HOW TO INCREASE THE RISK

The very act of having a plan creates risk. But there are several things an employer might do that increase risk.

Failure to maintain proper due diligence increases risk. According to ERISA attorney Ary Rosenbaum, while it is possible to outsource some responsibility, there is a catch in the wording "if an investment manager is properly appointed." In other words, an employer must approve and properly document the due diligence of this appointment for it to mitigate risk. According to Rosenbaum, many Plan Sponsors fail to do this and do not shift the liability they think they outsourced. The burden for due diligence is one reason it is important to work with an ERISA attorney.

Ignoring the rule to avoid conflicts of interest in the selection of service providers or investment options invites a great deal of risk. This falls into the category of not just avoiding improprieties but avoiding the very appearance of wrongdoing. A great example is what happened with the retirement plan at the Massachusetts Institute of Technology (MIT). The plan was using Fidelity, one of the largest recordkeeping service providers in the industry. It would be hard to argue that Fidelity does not provide an adequate solution for recordkeeping. But the fact that Fidelity's CEO, Abigail Johnson, sat on MIT's board of trustees appeared to be a conflict of interest, which did not help when MIT was sued over excessive fees. It led to the largest settlement ($18.1 million) challenging how universities manage their retirement plans.

The situation is not dissimilar from an employer hiring their bank to manage their 401(k) plan, or the owner hiring a brother-in-law to advise the 401(k), or any executive hiring a service provider after receiving gifts or paid vacations. It may not be a prohibitive transaction, and the bank or brother-in-law may provide the best solution, but it is clearly a conflict of interest, and you have an additional burden for due diligence to prove that there was not a better choice and that your decision was not unduly influenced.

The same goes for conflicts of interest involving investment options. In the MIT lawsuit, the investment fees were related to Fidelity funds. Anytime a Recordkeeper requires the use of their own proprietary investments, it creates a conflict of interest, just as in the case of an advisor who uses their own investments or portfolios that provide additional revenue. Conflicts of interest increase risk.

Failure to properly monitor service providers also increases risk. You should benchmark and evaluate your service providers every three to five years. This does not require changing service providers, but it does require evaluating them (and, if they fall short, a willingness to change providers...even if it is the brother-in-law).

Allowing additional services that increase cost also increases risk. The best example of this is allowing the plan advisor to implement Managed Accounts at an additional cost. Managed Accounts (MAs) are portfolios (sometimes constructed from investments in the underlying core fund list and sometimes constructed from outside investments). The Government Accountability Office denounced the use of MAs inside workplace retirement plans, concerned primarily with the additional cost.[5] Managed Accounts may add value, but it is hard to argue they warrant an additional cost, particularly when many providers offer MAs at no additional cost. Adding MAs for extra fees adds risk, particularly if the expensive MA option is the default investment.

And, finally, there are some practices conducted by insurance agents that add risk (practices in violation of most Education Policy Statements). For example, if the plan's

---

5   The US Government Accountability Office (GAO) issued the findings of a study (GAO-14-310) that discouraged the use of Managed Accounts inside workplace retirement plans. The primary concern of the study was cost. If your retirement plan offers an MA program or a custom-built Target Date Fund at no additional cost (which many service providers do today), the issue is not the same. You can read the full report of the government's warning about the Managed Accounts programs at gao.gov/products/GAO-14-310.

advisor is meeting with employees for education but also selling additional products to the employees, it increases your risk. The plan advisor should not solicit additional business, cross-sell annuities, or capture rollovers. Unleashing salespeople in the breakroom increases your risk. Your employees may feel pressured to buy additional products or, at the very least, believe you endorsed them. *"After all, if the boss hired this person to meet with me…what they're selling must be in my best interest."*

You must act in the best interest of plan participants, and allowing a sales pitch during 401(k) meetings increases your risk.

You have enough fiduciary risk when sponsoring a plan without making these additional blunders to increase that liability.

6

HIRING THE RIGHT ARCHITECT

THE ROLE (AND VALUE) OF A PLAN FIDUCIARY ADVISOR

The Kansas City Chiefs were a good football team in 2017. They had won their division two years in a row and had made the NFL playoffs three years in a row. But in the 2017 NFL draft, they selected Patrick Mahomes. He started in 2018, and in his first full year was the league MVP, only the second quarterback in NFL history to throw for 5,000 yards and 50 touchdowns in a season.[1] He took the Chiefs to the Conference Championship in 2018, won the Super Bowl in 2019, and took them back to the Super Bowl in 2020. At 24

---

[1] Peyton Manning was the other.

years of age, he may already be one of the best quarterbacks to ever play the position.

A great quarterback makes all the difference. They make everyone around them better. And a rising tide floats all boats.

Similarly, the right architect is the key to designing a successful plan. A workplace retirement plan has a lot of moving parts and layers of complexity. There are multiple players and duties to coordinate. It requires experience and expertise, and there is a ton of fiduciary liability. At the very least, a plan advisor is like a general contractor who coordinates the project. But the right advisor can be like a quarterback who makes everyone on the team better.

To design a retirement plan that serves your purpose and your people—a 401(k) plan that actually works—the plan fiduciary (the employer) needs a plan fiduciary advisor.

My advice is to only work with a consultant who will take a fiduciary role in writing. A plan fiduciary advisor does more than just advise the plan fiduciaries—they *are* a plan fiduciary—an ERISA 3(21) Co-Fiduciary or an ERISA 3(38) Investment Manager.

Anyone offering advice to an ERISA retirement plan is a fiduciary, but only engage advisors who are willing to put it in writing. Hiring a broker unwilling to sign on as a fiduciary is a waste of money because a plan fiduciary advisor must be a fiduciary.

THE PLAN FIDUCIARY ADVISOR SHOULD ALSO BE A SPECIALIST

A dedicated plan advisor is a professional consultant devoted to learning and maintaining the necessary competencies to serve workplace retirement plans. This involves an ongoing dedication to improving their craft and a lifelong commitment to continuing education in the subject matter of ERISA. The plan fiduciary advisor is not an ERISA attorney—nor are they a substitute for ERISA counsel—but they are subject matter experts in ERISA.

The guideline of prudence under ERISA indicates fiduciaries "unfamiliar with such matters" should "discharge their duties" to experts who are familiar. Anyone presenting themselves as a plan fiduciary advisor must have such expertise as a qualifying factor.

A financial professional may be completely competent with financial matters in general but be unacquainted with workplace retirement plans in particular. It would be akin to hiring a general practitioner to perform a highly specialized surgical procedure. An advisor who only dabbles in retirement plans is sometimes referred to as a "two-plan

Tony" or a "one-truck Chuck." It is completely fair to ask your advisor what percentage of their practice is dedicated to 401(k) business. Are retirement plans an afterthought or part of their core competencies?

The advisor you hire depends on what is important to you. Is expertise in plan design important? Is expertise in ERISA matters to maintain DOL compliance important? Is it important to find an advisor to serve the employees or the employer or both? Is a focus on Retirement Readiness that produces healthy outcomes important?

Admittedly, it may seem difficult to discern which financial professionals are qualified, but the difficulty does not dismiss your responsibility for due diligence in hiring a plan fiduciary advisor. And there are several key indicators of what to look for when making that selection.

For example, are they securities registered, and if so, which securities licenses do they carry? For instance, with Series 6, an individual can purchase or sell variable life insurance, municipal fund securities, variable annuities, mutual funds, and unit investment trusts. This license may indicate the financial professional is a nonspecialist. With a Series 65 or 66, on the other hand, an individual may offer investment advice as an Investment Advisor Representative (under the jurisdiction of a Registered Investment Adviser). This license is more likely to indicate the financial professional is a retirement plan specialist. None of these licenses specifically include or exclude services to workplace retirement plans, but some licenses permit financial professionals to broker financial products, while other licenses permit financial professionals to offer advice.

Another key indicator of what to look for when selecting financial professionals are designations and certifications. While no individual designation is required to perform the work, the focus of their practice is shown in the certificates they carry.

For example, a Certified Financial Planner™ (CFP®)[2] is the highest accreditation for individual financial planning, and a person would probably not want to hire a personal advisor without this accreditation. But plan advising is different than personal advising. A Certified Plan Fiduciary Advisor (CPFA®),[3] on the other hand, indicates expertise and experience with workplace retirement plans. This is not to disparage any designation or its recipients, each of whom qualified for the certification with that governing body's standards. But the designations emphasize the specialization of an advisor, most of whom make it super easy by listing the certifications in their signature.

---

2 The CFP® is a designation granted by the Certified Financial Planner Board of Standards, Inc.

3 The CPFA® is a designation granted by the National Association of Plan Advisors (NAPA). While membership in NAPA does not indicate any level of expertise, it does demonstrate an emphasis or focus for that financial professional's practice.

Designations that indicate specialization with insurance products include the Chartered Life Underwriter (CLU®), the Chartered Financial Consultant (ChFC®), the Certified Insurance Counselor (CIC®), the Certification for Long-Term Care (CLTC®), and the Retirement Income Certified Professional (RICP®).[4]

And designations that indicate specialization with individual investors include the Chartered Financial Analyst (CFA®) and the Accredited Wealth Management Advisor (AWMA®).

On the other hand, designations that indicate a specialty working with *institutional* retirement plans *in the workplace* (as opposed to individual retirement plans) include the aforementioned CPFA® as well as the Certified Investment Management Analyst (CIMA®), the Accredited Investment Fiduciary® (AIF®), the Accredited Investment Fiduciary Analyst® (AIFA®), the Certified Behavioral Finance Analyst (CBFA®), the C(k)P® Certified 401(k) Professional, the Chartered Retirement Plans Specialist (CRPS®), and the Certified Employee Benefits Specialist (CEBS).

None of the designations listed qualify the holder of these certificates—their expertise is ultimately grounded in their

---

[4] This list of insurance designations and certifications is not intended to be exhaustive but illustrative, nor is the inclusion of any designation herein intended to be an endorsement or disparagement of that certification or the designee upon whom it is granted.

experience in the industry—but the certifications listed above are indicators of their concentration. An advisor's focus might change, but if they are still listing professional "letters" after their name, this is still their focus. It is prudent for you to seek a financial professional who currently lists designations related to the duties of a plan fiduciary advisor—and *only* lists designations related to these duties—as it seems to indicate a specialization with 401(k)s.

THE PLAN FIDUCIARY ADVISOR SHOULD ALSO BE FEE-ONLY[5]

The primary duty of the plan fiduciary advisor is to offer advice, and the advice is conflicted if the advisor accepts commission payments. Removing conflicts of interest in a "fee-only" arrangement allows the advisor to truly do what is best for the client. Therefore, knowing how the advisor is paid is crucial in knowing for whom the advisor works.

Broadly speaking, there are essentially three different models within the financial industry.

1. The Captive Insurance Model
2. The Brokerage Firm Model
3. The Independent Advisory Model

---

[5] This section is a truncated version of Chapter 9 from my previous book, where the discussion was about the types of financial professionals offering personal advice, but the same guidance also applies to the types of financial professionals offering plan advice (Redstone, 2019).

"Captives" are insurance agents tasked with selling their firm's proprietary products. They are not working for their clients. They work for the insurance company. Their regulatory burden is to prove "suitability" for the products they sell. The agents are "held captive" because they sell a proprietary product. If they leave the agency, they must leave their clients (and commissions) behind.

The brokers are not held captive to an insurance company. But they are not selling advice; they are selling (brokering) financial products. They are Registered Representatives, or Registered Reps, paid commission for selling investment products. Brokers work for a commission check and need a "broker-dealer" (BD).

The Independent Advisory Model is different from the commission-based insurance models. These advisors are called Investment Adviser Representatives, and their firm is called a Registered Investment Adviser (RIA). Just as a broker needs a BD that reports to FINRA, the fee-only advisor needs an RIA that reports to the SEC.[6] These advisors are not paid commission. They are paid an advisory fee (an asset-based fee or a flat fee), their business is investment advice, and they are held to a "fiduciary standard," legally obligated to do what is *solely* in the best interest of the client.

---

6   FINRA is the Financial Industry Regulatory Authority, which provides oversight for brokers and broker-dealers. The SEC refers to the US Securities and Exchange Commission, which provides oversight for Investment Advisers under the Investment Advisers Act of 1940.

A person can discover the model of an advisor by looking at their disclosures. The disclosure will either reference "Registered Investment Adviser" (which is the third model) or it will say "Securities offered through _____" and possibly indicate that the organization is a member of FINRA/SIPC.[7] This is an indication that the advisor is operating in one of the first two models. (Note: Some financial advisors operate in a hybrid model, meaning they can work as a fee-based advisor or a commission-based broker. If they are wearing their fee-based hat, they are working for the client, but if they are wearing their broker hat, they are working for commissions.) My advice is to understand these three models, do some research, and do a background check. FINRA provides information about financial advisors from the first two models at brokercheck.finra.org. The SEC provides info about advisors at adviserinfo.sec.gov.

Look for a financial professional who is paid to provide advice and not to sell products, and a plan fiduciary advisor who is willing to be held to a fiduciary standard to operate in your best interest.

A 401(K) ARCHITECT SERVES BOTH SPONSORS AND PARTICIPANTS

A plan fiduciary advisor who serves the Plan Sponsor but ignores the plan participants will have trouble producing

---

[7] The Financial Industry Regulatory Authority and The Securities Investor Protection Corporation.

healthy retirement outcomes; conversely, an advisor who serves the plan participants but overlooks the fiduciary needs of the Plan Sponsor will have trouble keeping the plan in compliance. The 401(k) architect serves both and strikes a balance in designing the plan.

There are two primary service models with 401(k) plans: the boardroom versus the breakroom, or the pension model versus the insurance model. But a 401(k) architect follows a third model that balances both extremes.

Historically, the industry started with the pension model—with a focus on the employer in the boardroom. The employer retained the liability and assumed the risk because the employer was required to pay a "Defined Benefit" to employees upon retirement. The shift from Defined Benefit (DB) pension plans to Defined Contribution (DC) plans (like a 401k plan) was a shift in liability from the employer to the employees.

The financial industry also made a shift—a shift in focus from the boardroom to the breakroom—as the employees making the investment decisions became the focus. Unfortunately, employees also became the focus of sales under the insurance model.

The plan advisor had been an employee benefits consultant focused on the trustees of the plan, but when the conversation and focus shifted, the advisor was more likely to be an insurance agent intent on *making* clients of plan participants.

The first model is called the pension model even if the retirement plan is a 401(k); the name refers to the type of service provided rather than the type of retirement plan. The focus of the pension model is exclusively on the employer, and the plan fiduciary advisor meets with trustees in the boardroom rather than the employees in the breakroom. If employees receive help with their personal accounts, it is through education teams from the Recordkeeper.[8]

Similarly, the name of the other model—the insurance model—is also a colloquialism because it refers less to the insurance proffered and more to the sales focus on employees. The advisor only wants to stay in the boardroom long enough to be hired because the longer they are in the breakroom with employees, the more profitable the engagement. Plan participants receive a lot of help and one-on-one advice, but they also receive a sales pitch. If your Education Policy Statement allows salespeople in the breakroom, it can be quite profitable for the financial advisors. Financial reps may cross-sell services like Managed Accounts

---

8 This is education and not advice. In fact, the education teams are trained in how not to offer advice because it increases liability for the Recordkeeper. They can explain the plan, and sometimes they will administer a risk tolerance questionnaire to determine suitability, but they may not offer investment advice.

within the plan or products like life insurance outside the plan; they may help employees roll their money out of the 401(k) plan into an Individual Retirement Account (IRA); and they may even roll it into a guaranteed annuity. Capturing rollovers—harvesting profits by rolling money out of the workplace retirement plan and into an IRA with higher fees—is a conflict of interest. Some 401(k) plans allow in-service withdrawals for employees over 59½ years of age, and some advisors focus their attention on this age group. The conflict of interest exists when the advisor stands to make more on money leaving the plan than staying in the plan; it prejudices their advice.

Ultimately, both models have their strengths and weaknesses. Workplace retirement plans served by the pension model are more likely to be in compliance, though studies show participation rates and savings rates lag without attention from advisors on the employees. On the other hand, workplace retirement plans served by the insurance model may have higher participation rates with more people saving more money, though the plan faces regulatory issues when the advisor is not a specialist in fiduciary matters.

Sometimes plan size influences the service model. Larger entities are more likely to utilize the pension model; smaller groups are more likely to utilize the insurance model. This may be due to logistics—it is more difficult to do one-on-one breakroom meetings with thousands of employees. Or this may be due to competencies—more sophisticated Plan Sponsors[9] are less likely to hire a nonspecialist advisor who understands less about the regulatory environment than they do. But regardless of size, trustees in the boardroom need help, and employees in the breakroom need help.

The 401(k) architect has emerged as a third option—a balance between both models that serves both audiences. The RPC needs a specialist sitting in the room, and the employees need attention from the plan advisor without a sales pitch to cross-sell additional financial products.

My recommendation for the third model is based on extensive experience from all angles, including working as a financial professional for years in both models. When I started my career, I worked directly with plan participants for a Recordkeeper. In that role, I was not allowed to offer advice; my job was education, not advice. I could explain to employees how their plan worked, but I was not allowed to make recommendations. After a lengthy (compliance-approved) script, the question employees asked was, "Okay, so what should I do?"...but I was forbidden to answer.

---

9   Not that they are specialized in being a Plan Sponsor, but that they are employed by a Plan Sponsor that is large enough to allow for specialization and expertise. For example, at a smaller employer, there might be one person who is responsible for all HR matters, while a larger employer might have hundreds of employees in their HR department, dozens in the benefits segment of the HR department, and a few individuals whose entire job at work is managing the 401(k) plan. In these instances, the Plan Sponsor is not an HR generalist and may know more about workplace retirement plans than many advisors who call on them, particularly if the advisors are not highly experienced specialists themselves.

In my next job, I ran the retirement advisory practice for a large life insurance agency and later a regional financial agency. At both jobs, we operated in the insurance model, providing advice in the breakroom. I saw the good (higher participation and savings) and the bad (cross-selling) and the ugly (cannibalizing the 401k to capture rollovers). Employees thrived with one-on-one attention, but it is hard to deny the true reason the agencies were in the 401(k) business: additional sales in the breakroom.

After working in the insurance model, I shifted to the pension model as a partner with the largest independent consulting firm in the world. The clients of our firm were exclusively institutional—commercial property and casualty insurance, group health, and workplace retirement plans—with a focus on the boardroom and not the breakroom. The decision was made to *not* engage employees within the plan, to *not* solicit rollovers or offer advice. We had no contact with employees whatsoever. Advisors in the insurance model were aggressively pursuing interaction with plan participants, but at our firm, we were just as aggressively prohibiting interaction. A client contacted us during the Recession to request employee meetings—they didn't want us to send the Recordkeeper's educators; they wanted meetings with our advisors—and we denied the request! Another partner at the firm said, "We don't meet with employees," as if meeting with them implied cross-selling. I was not offering to meet with employees to sell them anything; I was offering to meet with them to calm their fears and offering to meet at the client's request.

The point is, I have experienced the models, and I have seen their strengths and weaknesses. I served in the small to micro market, the mid to large market, and even in the jumbo market with billion-dollar retirement plans. I served on the Recordkeeper side of the table and the advisor side of the table. As a financial professional, I worked in the captive insurance model, the brokerage firm model, and the independent RIA model. And as a plan fiduciary advisor, I served in the insurance model and the pension model, serving the breakroom and the boardroom.

Learning from the pros and cons of each of these positions, today our firm operates as an independent RIA with a balanced approach to serving both the boardroom and the breakroom. The one-on-one employee meetings are key to fostering better engagement and producing healthy outcomes. And meeting individually with participants to offer advice does not mean cross-selling or soliciting additional products—it means helping you build a workplace retirement plan that produces healthy outcomes.

Based on my experience, it works best when the plan fiduciary advisor is a fee-only, qualified specialist who serves both the boardroom and the breakroom, a professional who understands clearly that the employer is the "client," while never venturing to make a "client" of plan participants.

If the goal is to design a healthy workplace retirement plan that serves your purpose and your people, a 401(k) architect can help you get there.

A list of the top plan fiduciary advisors in the industry can be found at retirementadvisor.us. And this link to the "Member Advisor Map" can help you find an advisor in your region: retirementadvisor.us/homepage/member-advisor-map.

POURING THE FOUNDATION

USING THE RIGHT PLATFORM AND TOOLS TO BUILD THE PLAN

In a construction project, every element plays a crucial part in the process—walls, roof, plumbing, and wiring—but perhaps no portion of the project is more vital to success than the foundation.

A smart builder builds their house on solid rock—fixed to a firm foundation—so that nothing moves it, as opposed to the house of cards that collapses when the storm rolls in.

In designing and building a 401(k), the service providers—Recordkeeper and Administrator—provide the platform. So, after hiring the 401(k) architect, pouring a solid foundation with the service provider paves the way for your success.

A 401(k) architect can help you evaluate the various services and platforms, understand which features are important to have on hand, and recommend the best fit for your unique workplace.

EVALUATING SERVICES AND PLATFORMS

There are a variety of services and service providers with the workplace retirement plan,[1] but the two primary functions are recordkeeping and administration. Some consider recordkeeping services to be primary, as the most visible provider (especially to employees), but the administrative services are key to making the plan work and keeping the plan in compliance.

The Recordkeeper is primarily tasked with keeping records for the plan and records of each account within the plan. To facilitate this function, Recordkeepers maintain a web portal to access accounts. Recordkeepers also prepare

---

[1] Examples of additional service providers not discussed in this book include custodial services, trustee services, and ERISA auditors. The custodian is like a bank, with custody of the money in the plan. Sometimes there is an additional custodial fee, but often the cost of custodial services is included within other fees. Employers generally do not have a choice of custodians; it is the Recordkeeper's decision about where they bank. The employer does have a choice, however, to be a self-trustee or add a corporate trustee at additional cost. And while the employer does not have a choice about whether to have an ERISA audit (determined by the number of eligible employees) the employer does have a choice about which audit firm to hire.

and deliver statements to the employees. Generally, the Recordkeeper will also prepare enrollment and education materials, facilitate the onboarding of eligible participants, and subsequently handle distributions for terminated participants. Other service providers, like Administrators and custodians, are behind the scenes and unknown to most plan participants.

The administrative services are distinctly different than recordkeeping services and may be provided by the Recordkeeper or by a TPA. In other words, the same service provider may perform both recordkeeping and administration in what is called a "bundled solution." But sometimes the Recordkeeper is unable to perform the administrative tasks and requires an outside administrator (TPA) in what is called an "unbundled solution." The recordkeeping services are always ministerial or non-fiduciary, meaning that the Recordkeeper is an "order taker." They follow the direction of your employees about investment decisions, your direction about plan design, and even the direction of the TPA about interpretations of the Plan Document. In their ministerial role, the Recordkeeper never makes plan decisions.

Adding an outside administrator may add cost but not value. You should only add a TPA if it adds value, and the primary value an outside administrator adds is when operating in a nonministerial role as an ERISA 3(16) Administrative

Fiduciary. In other words, all the recordkeeping services are ministerial, and some of the administrative services are ministerial, but some of the administrative services are also fiduciary in nature. The TPA, if not a fiduciary, does not have to take legal responsibility for any of their administration, but an Administrative Fiduciary can and will take legal responsibility for administration.

One option is to use the same company for both recordkeeping and administration. Another option is to separate out the administration *for the purpose of hiring an Administrative Fiduciary*.

The administrative services include accounting tasks that are ministerial in nature, such as compliance testing for nondiscrimination and contribution limits; preparation of the Form 5500 filing; tracking the money for contributions, forfeitures, and distributions; and calculating vesting. But administrative services also include functions that are more than merely ministerial in nature, such as maintaining the plan document, plan amendments, and restatements. And administrative services can include functions that are fiduciary in nature, such as signing and filing Form 5500, interpreting plan provisions for the Recordkeeper, and preparing and delivering participant notices.

An ERISA 3(16) Administrative Fiduciary shifts the greatest amount of liability away from you because most compliance issues are administrative in nature (making timely deposits or delivery of required employee notices). If the administrator prepares Form 5500, but you sign it, you retain the legal responsibility for whether it is correct; if the administrator prepares it, signs it, and files it, the administrator mitigates an enormous amount of liability. If you add a second company to handle administrative functions in an unbundled environment, hire a TPA performing fiduciary services in addition to the ministerial services.

Recordkeeping and administration are handled by a variety of service providers, but, generally speaking, the administrators fall into one of two categories, while the Recordkeepers fall into one of three categories.[2] The administrators are either large regional or national firms that can accept fiduciary responsibility or small local TPAs that (generally) do not accept a fiduciary role. Meanwhile, Recordkeepers are (generally) banks, money managers, and insurance companies. Each of these platforms has pros and cons.

Sometimes banks provide recordkeeping services, though the number of national banks in recordkeeping continues to dwindle because it is difficult for recordkeeping to be profitable. The margins are thin, and profitability requires

---

[2] I say "generally speaking" because new providers (particularly in the fintech, or financial tech, space) periodically try to offer new solutions. If they do not reach enough scale to be profitable, they fail. Similarly, a few payroll companies have tried to provide recordkeeping solutions.

an enormous number of plan participants. Regional banks might also provide recordkeeping, though they probably lack the resources their national brethren have for investments in cybersecurity. National and regional banks can provide a good platform if they do not require their own proprietary funds. An example of a regional bank that provides recordkeeping is the Bank of Oklahoma (BOK Financial), while an example of a national bank that provides recordkeeping is JPMorgan Chase (although JPMorgan also manages investments, bridging the bank category and the money manager category).[3]

A second category of Recordkeepers consists of money managers or Investment Managers. Their primary business is managing investments, and the recordkeeping business is a distribution channel for their investments. To combat the thin margins and provide recordkeeping at a profitable rate, they might require the use of proprietary funds. There are primarily four money managers that provide both investments and recordkeeping: Fidelity, Vanguard, T. Rowe Price, and American Funds.[4]

The third and most prevalent category of Recordkeepers consists of insurance companies. Historically, many insurance companies entered this space by building group

---

[3] This example is not an endorsement. This service provider and the others mentioned throughout this section are for illustration purposes only.

[4] Neither is this example an endorsement.

annuities, essentially group insurance products. The underlying investments were separately managed accounts rather than mutual funds with NAV pricing,[5] and fees were "hidden" inside the insurance policy in a "wrap fee."[6] Some insurance companies now offer a trust platform with real mutual funds in addition to their group annuities, and most insurance companies have reduced the expensive wraps, moving toward greater fee disclosure. Whether reacting to the pressure from "fee compression" or proactively adopting fair fee pricing, insurance companies providing recordkeeping have improved dramatically. Historically, insurance companies were the most expensive option, but today, insurance companies may provide the lowest-cost option, even doing creative rebates that mutual fund companies and trust platforms cannot offer, like returning foreign tax credits within the group annuities. Examples of insurance companies providing recordkeeping abound, including Empower, John Hancock, Nationwide, Principal, Securian, TIAA, Transamerica, VALIC, Voya, and so on.[7]

---

5   Net asset value (NAV) represents a fund's per share cost. The NAV computation is undertaken once at the end of each trading day based on the closing market prices of the portfolio's securities.

6   Wrap fees allow financial institutions to bundle together a variety of different services, including management expenses, trading costs, sub-TA (sub-transfer agency) fees, and 12b-1 fees (traditionally designed for marketing and paid to advisors receiving a commission). Wrapping all the fees into an asset-based fee was supposed to make things as simple as possible for investors, but it also made hiding the fees possible for service providers. The relatively high level of some wrap fees has earned scrutiny from regulators.

7   Again, this is not meant to be a comprehensive list nor an endorsement of any particular insurance company that provides recordkeeping. These providers are listed alphabetically, and multiple providers were left off the list.

Selecting the right platform upon which to build the plan starts with understanding the differences between the service providers.

UNDERSTANDING DIFFERENT FEATURES OF THE SERVICE PROVIDERS

Some Recordkeepers appear to be identical, even offering similar tools and similar-looking web portals.[8] But there are subtle differences between Recordkeepers that an experienced 401(k) architect can help you understand before laying the foundation.

A big differentiator, of course, is whether the service provider is a bank, mutual fund company, or insurance company. Another demarcation is whether the service provider will take a fiduciary role or operate in a non-fiduciary capacity. Still another point of comparison between service providers is size, because larger Recordkeepers may have more resources to invest in technology and the cybersecurity to protect the technology. Another area of contrast is with the investment options themselves: not all funds are available on all platforms. Another difference is whether the Recordkeeper's pricing is self-sustaining and profit-

---

8   One explanation for this is that many Recordkeepers use the same software programs rather than building custom applications. Another reason for this is that some Recordkeepers literally provide recordkeeping services for other Recordkeepers. For example, Empower owns FASCore, which provides recordkeeping for other companies, like JPMorgan.

able, or whether recordkeeping is a loss leader for ancillary revenue streams. (Most recordkeeping is NOT profitable.)

Before a mutual fund can be offered on a recordkeeping platform, the Recordkeeper must have a selling agreement in place with the mutual fund company. Some platforms offer a very limited number of investment options, although it is still entirely possible to build a diversified portfolio from among the options available.

Some Recordkeepers have proprietary fund requirements, whether they require plans to use their registered mutual funds or require plans to use their general account for the cash option. Other Recordkeepers are completely "open architecture" with no proprietary fund requirements, although you should note that truly open architecture platforms are rare. Some Recordkeepers may claim to be open architecture because they do not manage mutual funds (meaning they have no proprietary funds and therefore no proprietary fund requirement) and yet their platform (a) does not offer access to *all* investment options or (b) requires the use of their own stable value or stable asset. Other Recordkeepers, if they manage mutual funds, have preferential pricing for plans that use their funds; they allow you to use other funds but at an additional cost. To be clear, this is not wrong—it is not wrong for a company to provide better pricing if using their funds—but it is something to be aware of and to be properly disclosed.

It is better if you are not beholden to the Recordkeeper. The Recordkeeper exists to serve you, as the plan fiduciary. The RPC monitors investments according to the IPS, not according to the proprietary fund restrictions. If a fund fails the IPS criteria, it must be removed, even if it is a proprietary fund of the Recordkeeper. Restricting your ability to make fund changes inhibits your fiduciary responsibility and may create a compliance issue if it requires the retention of underperforming investments. You should have the ability to pick any fund that fits the IPS—or replace any fund that does not fit the IPS—without restriction and without adjusting cost.

Therefore, finding the best fit starts with picking funds first.

FINDING THE BEST FIT FOR EACH WORKPLACE

Let me be clear in saying there is not one size that fits all.[9] There is not a single service provider with the perfect solution for every workplace retirement plan. Some Recordkeepers provide a great solution for small plans, others specialize in larger plans, and others specialize in multiple plans with layers of complexity. Some providers specialize in 401(k) plans and others specialize in 403(b)

---

9   A possible indicator of an inexperienced or nonspecialized plan advisor is when they offer the same recordkeeping solution for every employer. No service provider is perfect for every situation. But a nonspecialist, unfamiliar with other providers, is limited in their solutions. This advisor is a "one-trick pony." Unfortunately, a "two-plan Tony" is often a one-trick pony, because limited experience with serving plans results in limited solutions.

plans. There are Recordkeepers that emphasize fiduciary services, while others emphasize education services. Some specialize in state-of-the-art technology, while others provide a higher level of personal service. And some invest enormous amounts in cybersecurity to protect the technology and your data, while other, smaller providers lack the resources. The right platform depends on your culture and your needs.

Ultimately, what you need is flexibility and customization.

Start by hiring a 401(k) architect who can work with *any* platform to find the right foundation to design your plan. Conversely, the platform should be able to accommodate *any* investment: no restrictions, no limits, and complete flexibility, which allows for greater customization to find the right fit.

To avoid restrictions and limitations, work with a 401(k) architect to select the funds first (or at least to select the professionally managed portfolio option first). A 401(k) architect, for example, starts with a Glidepath Optimization Analysis™ to select the optimal glidepath for your unique employee population. A glidepath[10] is the portfolio allocation for each employee as they progress toward retirement,

---

10   Glidepaths are explained further in the next chapter. The term references the "gliding" or diminishing amount of equity exposure (exposure to the stock market) as a plan participant ages. Traditionally, glidepaths were the dominion of Target Date Funds, but, increasingly, the glidepath might be a customized age-based portfolio your 401(k) architect builds.

and it varies for each employee, as it does for each employer, based upon industry, average age of your employees, average money saved thus far in the 401(k), and several other factors. Identifying the appropriate glidepath determines whether a custom glidepath needs to be built or an existing Target Date Fund fits. And if using an existing allocation of funds, that determines the Recordkeeper to choose.

For example, if the Glidepath Optimization Analysis™ indicates that you should use the JPMorgan Target Date Funds[11] or Fidelity Target Date Funds,[12] it makes sense to consider using JPMorgan or Fidelity for recordkeeping, or at least a Recordkeeper who allows their funds. Using the same company for both investments and recordkeeping might save money. Select the funds first, and then identify a Recordkeeper that fits the funds. Selecting the *Recordkeeper* first might mean you are stuck with funds that do not fit.

However, it is always preferable to have recordkeeping cost unassociated with investments. After all, the funds that fit today may not fit tomorrow, and if removing those funds adversely impacts recordkeeping fees, you may wish you

---

11 This is *not* a recommendation, an endorsement, or a criticism of the Target Date Funds from JPMorgan, also known as the JPMorgan SmartRetirement funds. This is merely an example for illustration purposes.

12 This is *not* a recommendation, an endorsement, or a criticism of the Target Date Funds from Fidelity, also known as the Fidelity Freedom Funds. This is merely an example for illustration purposes.

had hired a Recordkeeper independent from the use of any proprietary funds.

SEQUENCING MATTERS

Imagine how big a miscalculation it might be if *you* started building your house, and then *you* purchased your supplies, and then you hired the builder who was limited to using your supplies, and then you hired the architect to design a house already started. Building backward is unlikely to be a formula for success. And yet this is a common mistake some employers make: hiring the Recordkeeper first, getting stuck with proprietary funds provided by the Recordkeeper, and then hiring a plan advisor...or not hiring an advisor at all.

Perhaps you work directly with your Recordkeeper, without the assistance of a plan advisor, because you thought the advisor's role an unnecessary duplication or an unnecessary cost. But when a plan fiduciary is working without a plan fiduciary advisor, it adds fiduciary liability, liability the Recordkeeper does not assume in the absence of an advisor. Nor does the Recordkeeper provide the hands-on service of a local advisor. But the greatest irony is that adding a plan advisor may *not* add cost and may even save cost. Adding a fiduciary advisor should add *value* but could be cost-neutral.

I have started multiple engagements with companies that had previously worked directly with their Recordkeeper, but *after* they hired us, we decreased the cost. One reason is because the share class of investments was higher than necessary. Another reason is because the recordkeeping was overpriced, and they needed an advocate to negotiate better pricing. At other times, the Recordkeeper was including cost for services not even utilized. For example, the contract included on-site education, but the employer rarely used all the days for which they were billed. A local advisor can deliver employee meetings more consistently and affordably, providing financial advice the Recordkeeper is not allowed to offer.

My experience is that some Recordkeepers collect more in fees than they need to operate the plan—and offer less service—but rather than refunding the excess, some Recordkeepers pocket the difference. A plan fiduciary advisor may save you money.

Finding the best fit and laying a solid foundation begins with engaging a qualified 401(k) architect to design and build the right plan. The Recordkeeper provides the platform and the tools you need, but the 401(k) architect brings it all together. A plan fiduciary advisor ensures the plan is built on the appropriate foundation.

8

PLAN FEES

BUILDING A GREAT PLAN WITHOUT PAYING A GREAT PRICE

In construction projects, cost overruns are relatively common. In fact, excess costs are so commonplace that most construction loans have overage protection built in. Not surprisingly, when projects are awarded to the lowest bid, some estimates are unsustainable. Inaccurate estimates, serious project design errors, and poor management all lead to overruns. It is a typical business practice in the construction industry, and we just accept it.

What we cannot accept are overruns in the retirement industry. You may accept overages on the construction of your office building, but you must not accept overages on the construction of benefits programs for your employees who work in the office building. After all, overruns on the facility are paid by the company, but overruns on employee benefits are (generally) paid by the employees. Overpaying on 401(k) fees is unacceptable, particularly because it is not your money to pay (or overpay). As a sponsor of the plan, you have a burden to ensure the fees are appropriate.

But building a great plan does not require paying a great price.

This chapter outlines the legal responsibility for monitoring fees, itemizes and identifies the real cost in building a plan, and provides advice about appropriate benchmarks.

THE REGULATORY REQUIREMENTS CONCERNING PLAN FEES

ERISA says the fiduciary burden is to act in the best interest of plan participants. Only certain reasonable costs may be covered by plan assets,[1] and even then, you have a responsibility to make sure employees are not overpaying. In an effort at greater disclosure and accountability, the regulators[2]

---

[1] This section is not intended to provide legal advice, particularly in regard to which costs may legally be paid from plan assets. Please consult ERISA counsel as it pertains to your particular retirement plan.

[2] ERISA (the Employee Retirement Income Security Act of 1974) is governed and amended by Congress. The fiduciary guidelines of ERISA are enforced by the Department of Labor (DOL), or more specifically the Employee Benefits Security Administration (EBSA) within the DOL. And the tax guidelines of ERISA are enforced by the IRS. Therefore, "regulators" could apply to Congress, the DOL, or the IRS, and plans may be audited by the DOL or the IRS.

established two reporting requirements: ERISA 404(a)5 and ERISA 408(b)2.

29 CFR § 2550.404a-5—Participant Disclosures—The regulations require that employees be provided transparency about the investment options, with regard to cost and performance, prior to enrollment and then on an annual basis. This requirement is not difficult to meet and is most generally covered by the Recordkeeper with the participant statements each quarter.

29 CFR § 2550.408b-2—Service Provider Disclosures— The regulations require that employers be provided transparency about the service providers serving their retirement plan, with regard to cost and fiduciary status, on at least on an annual basis. This requirement is evidently more difficult to meet, as evidenced by the failures of most service providers (and most retirement plans).

The guidelines require every "Covered Service Provider" (a service provider that receives more than $1,000 in compensation) make explicit disclosures to the retirement plans they serve. Specifically, the disclosures must contain four essential elements:

1. Who the service provider is
2. A description of the services provided
3. A declaration of the fiduciary status of the provider

PLAN FEES · 165

4. The fee or expense charged by the provider

The 408b-2 regulation specifically says that *every* Covered Service Provider (CSP) must provide their disclosures on at least an annual basis so that the employer might ascertain whether the fees are fair, reasonable, and necessary.

It would be prudent of the Retirement Plan Committee to establish a Disclosure Policy Statement (DPS) to mitigate liability by outlining how 408b-2 will be addressed, since many plans fall short.

One of the ways 408b-2 is violated is with the CSP provision. In fact, it is *uncommon* for every provider to deliver adequate annual disclosures. The largest providers, like the Recordkeeper, generally comply, but other providers, like the broker, may not, though they receive more than $1,000 in compensation. Typically, you receive one 408b-2 disclosure—not one from each provider, but one. It is the responsibility of each provider, though you as the Plan Sponsor are liable for noncompliance.

Further complicating the disclosure requirement is the lack of standardized reporting. For example, the DOL requested certain information and standardized how it should be reported with Form 5500. But in the case of 408b-2, regulators requested certain information but stopped short of standardizing how it should be reported. Broad interpretation allows the disclosures from some providers to be clear, while others are unnecessarily complex. The purpose of 408b-2 was transparency and clarity, yet many employers are still unclear on exactly what they pay. Standardized reporting would have enhanced the goal for transparency and kept some service providers from disguising their fees.

My recommendation is a form where the asset-based percentage and dollar amount are reported for investment fees, recordkeeping fees, advisory fees, and so on. And investment fees should be the actual weighted expense ratio based on where assets are allocated and how much was paid to the Recordkeeper and other providers. The lack of standardized reporting exacerbates noncompliance with 408b-2.

And, finally, the lack of benchmarking ensures noncompliance. The regulations do not require the cheapest possible solution but do require that plan fees be fair, reasonable, and necessary, which implies benchmarking. How else can you *ascertain* if the fees are fair, reasonable, and necessary in these four examples?

1. A 401(k) pays little for recordkeeping but receives little.
2. Another pays more but receives much more for their fee.
3. Another 401(k) pays for services (like on-site education days) that they do not receive.

4. And another 401(k) is dirt cheap but never benchmarks fees or services.

The first plan may be out of compliance; the second plan (paying more) *may* be in compliance, if properly benchmarked; the third plan (paying for unnecessary services) is out of compliance; and the fourth plan (without benchmarking) is out of compliance.

Perfect compliance with 408b-2 is rare; violations are common with CSP, reporting, and benchmarking. Regulators and service providers share in the blame and should share in the responsibility of fixing this to make sure the retirement plan does not have overruns. We must ensure plan fees are appropriate when they come out of the pocket of our employees.

IDENTIFYING THE REAL COST IN BUILDING A PLAN

Within workplace retirement plans, there are multiple components related to cost and an array of entities seeking to be paid, although outsourcing services does not mean increasing cost. More cooks in the kitchen should not result in a more expensive meal.

And greater disclosure helps. Who pays whom and how much?

Generally, plan expenses fall into three categories: plan administration fees, participant transaction fees, and investment fees.

Plan administration fees are expenses associated with maintenance and service to the plan, to the plan's trustees, and to the plan's participants. Any cost of administering the plan falls into this broad category. It involves things like recordkeeping services, administrative services, audit services, custodial services, accounting services, trustee services, 3(16) services, and even advisory services (3.21 or 3.38 services). Plan administration fees may be paid as a flat fee or asset-based fee or per-head fee, and paid from plan assets (meaning plan participants pay the fee) or paid directly by you, the employer. All these service providers are paid, but rarely is it completely transparent how much each entity is paid, as some are subcontractors. For example, the Recordkeeper charges a fee for maintaining records, maintaining the website, and sending statements, but they do not actually have custody of the money. The custodian is a bank with whom the Recordkeeper partners, and the custodian charges an additional fee, generally paid by the Recordkeeper.

To be clear, I am not critiquing this business practice, nor am I denying any provider their right to payment for services rendered. I am simply using this illustration as an example of the lack of transparency. And while it can be terribly confusing, the solution is simple: regulators should standardize a form that requires complete disclosure.[3] Because the administrative fees are not clear, it manifests distrust. The plan fees may be quite fair, entirely reasonable, and completely necessary, but when you do not understand the fees, you naturally become suspicious.

Participant transaction fees are expenses for optional services provided on an individual participant basis. Participant transaction fees may be paid as a flat fee or asset-based fee. They are paid by your employees requesting the transaction or service. You do not pay the fee, nor does it come out of plan assets in the sense that all employees pay the fee. Only the individual employee effecting the transaction or service pays the fee. And yet, you as the plan fiduciary are responsible for ensuring your employees are not overpaying. One example of a participant transaction fee is a distribution fee. And if, for example, the distribution fee is outrageously priced, you have culpability in not monitoring fees to safeguard against unreasonableness. Another example of a participant transaction fee is a Managed Accounts fee. Again, as with loan fees, only the employee receiving this service pays the fee, but this does not excuse you from

---

[3] A standardized form requires every provider to report the same information in the same manner, promoting clarity and preventing deception. An example might look like this: "On line 17, write the actual dollar amount paid in recordkeeping fees last year...on line 18, write the recordkeeping fees as a percentage of plan assets...on line 19, write the custodial fees...total lines 17 through 20, unless custodial fees are included in recordkeeping fees."

the responsibility to monitor the fee. If the fee is excessive or if a lower-cost option or free alternative is available, you are liable for allowing fees to be charged to your employees if fees are unfair or unnecessary,[4] even if the fees are deemed optional.

Investment fees, on the other hand, are not optional. The cost connected with investment funds in the retirement plan (also called the expense ratio) is typically the largest expense to the plan and likely pays multiple service providers. These are asset-based fees, a percentage of the amount of money invested in each fund, paid by the plan participants. You, as the plan fiduciary, are responsible for ensuring your employees are not overpaying for the investment options, monitoring the expense ratio by controlling the share class, and understanding the all-in cost with how much is paid to various "subcontractors." It sounds easy enough, but the investment fees are...complicated.

For example, if one fund charges 0.50% while another fund charges 1.00%, a comparison of the two investments must also include performance because investment returns are

---

[4] With the prevalence of free Managed Accounts programs available in the market, it might be argued that any cost at all is unfair. Multiple Recordkeepers have developed programs that diversify allocations from among the core funds in the investment lineup at no additional cost, simply because they know that diversified portfolios benefit them, their clients, and their clients' employees. A few national firms have developed Managed Accounts, like Financial Engines, for an additional cost, although the cost varies as the assets increase past certain breakpoints. And a few regional or smaller RIA firms have developed Managed Accounts for much higher fees, 50, 100, or even 150 basis points. Paying 100 basis points (1%) for a service that is also available for free is unnecessary and unreasonable.

shown after fees have been deducted.[5] If the first fund had a return of 3% while the second fund had a return of 10%, the second fund had a much better return on investment. In this illustration, the management team of the second fund gained 11% in the market, kept 1% (the expense ratio) for their management, and reported 10% (the performance return) to the account holder. Since performance is shown after the fees are withdrawn, investment fees must be considered in the context of returns.

The real question is not in comparing two completely different funds but in comparing two share classes of the same fund.

Share classes are designations applied to types of investments, like mutual funds. Each share class is a different version of the same investment. However, the fees for each share class differ, and because the expense ratio is deducted prior to returns, the fee impacts performance. For example, a mutual fund may come in different share classes, sometimes a dozen or more: A shares, B shares, and C shares (traditionally called retail share classes); I shares and N shares (traditionally called the institutional share class); or retirement shares (R1, R2, R3, R4, R5, and R6). Different share classes—different versions—of the same fund. The only difference between them is the cost. Some

---

[5] This is commonly referred to as "net of fees" in the industry.

share classes have higher fees because they pay more service providers.

The investment fees are broken down into three categories: investment management fees (paid to the Investment Managers who manage the fund), sub-TA or sub-transfer agency fees (paid to the Recordkeeper for access to that platform), and 12b-1 marketing fees (or revenue sharing paid as commission to the plan's financial advisor or broker).

As an example, a fund manager (or management team) does the research to decide what to invest in, and they collect the investment management fee for managing the portfolio. The team may also pay the Recordkeeper for access to the platform, covered by the sub-TA fees, and commission to an insurance broker to sell the fund on that platform, covered by the 12b-1 marketing fees.

It is not important for you to understand all the nuances of plan fees, but it is crucial to have a basic understanding of total plan costs, as well as a thorough understanding of how much each service provider charges, to benchmark fees. For example, the plan advisor may be paid through plan administration fees (as an asset-based fee or as a flat fee), through participant transaction fees (from Managed Accounts), and through the investment fees (from 12b-1 commission). In other words, the same advisor may receive compensation on the same plan from all three sources.

The better you understand the fee structure and the cost of services, the better equipped you are to fulfill your fiduciary responsibility to monitor and benchmark plan fees.

ADVICE ABOUT BENCHMARKS AND CONTROLLING COST

I am not in favor of fee compression, just complete and transparent fee disclosure. Service providers should not hide or disguise their cost. In fact, if the fees are fair and reasonable, the services exchanged for those fees constitute an equitable transaction. You need to receive the information to determine if fees are fair, reasonable, and necessary.

Building a great plan does not mean paying a great price. But it does mean paying *some* price because none of these service providers work for free. And yet, I continue to hear, "We don't pay anything for recordkeeping," because employees do not see a line item for this service. (The Recordkeeper was probably paid excess revenue from investment fees, maybe even proprietary funds from the same Recordkeeper.) Recordkeepers are *not* nonprofits. But when it comes to cost, how much is enough, how much is too much, and how are you to know the difference?

My advice about plan fees is summarized in four tenets:

1. Nothing is free, and no one is working for free.
2. You get what you pay for.
3. Flat fees help you control how much you pay.
4. Benchmarking helps you compare how much you pay.

The idea that a service provider is working for nothing, or even working for markedly less than the competition, is absurd. If it looks like they are working for nothing, you have not identified all the fees. Or if their stated fee is absurdly small, they may be receiving compensation through another means. Or their plan level fees may be low because they hope to make additional revenue from cross-selling other products. The tradeoff is turning the enrollment meeting into a sales meeting, which increases the liability for you if you invite brokers to make a sales pitch to your employees. Some advisors refer to their 401(k) business as a "loss leader" because it puts them in front of individuals to cross-sell.

And you get what you pay for. Picking the cheapest funds, for instance, might be accepting the lowest returns. The returns are net of the fees, so investment fees are not the concern, but *overlay costs* come out after returns (things like a Managed Accounts fee or the Contract Asset Charge).

Flat fees were traditionally the pricing model for the administrators: a per-employee fee or a per-participant fee. But some Recordkeepers have begun to adopt a flat per-head fee rather than an asset-based fee. And some plan fiduciary advisors have moved to a flat-fee model (moving from commission to asset-based fees and eventually from asset-based fees to a flat fee).

Flat-fee pricing enhances greater transparency and facilitates better disclosure, but it also helps the plan fiduciary control the cost of their workplace retirement plan. An advisor might charge a fee in basis points (a percentage of plan assets) or a flat fee. The flat fee remains the same as plan assets increase, so, over time, the cost drops *as a percentage of assets*. Those who charge a flat fee will generally guarantee the fee for a defined period, allowing for occasional renegotiation as deemed appropriate.

Critics of the flat-fee pricing model argue they should benefit from the growth of the plan. Some ERISA attorneys, however, believe it is hard to defend charging more to serve the plan if the employer did not add more employees or more locations.

And finally, without a good reference point, comparing plan fees is merely guesswork. Fiduciaries should benchmark the cost of their advisor from an independent source (not another advisor). An entire industry has developed in recent years to facilitate better information, to make you an informed buyer. Benchmarking is important, and, at times, it is even advisable to pay for an independent benchmarking report.

The plan fiduciary advisor should help you benchmark other service providers. After all, your advisor is also a fiduciary with the same legal responsibility to ensure that fees are fair, reasonable, and necessary. A trusted plan fiduciary advisor can be your greatest asset in drafting and implementing your Disclosure Policy Statement, maintaining compliance with ERISA 408(b)2, and even renegotiating service contracts with other vendors to the plan.

The 401(k) architect designs a plan that stays on schedule and on budget. Then the architect applies "choice architecture" to help your employees and "goals-based architecture" to add plan features for your employees. In the next two chapters, we turn to these matters of plan design, the heart of 401(k) architecture.

9

KEEP IT SIMPLE

USING CHOICE ARCHITECTURE TO HELP YOUR EMPLOYEES

The coronavirus pandemic of 2020 exposed millions of Americans to both our physical and financial frailty—with more than 39 million confirmed cases[1] of COVID-19 but twice as many filing for unemployment.[2] But the biggest issue for some became the mandate to wear masks. Americans hate being told what to do, and this felt a little bit too much like Big Brother,[3] a little too paternalistic. There was

---

1   As of August 31, 2021, the confirmed cases in the US surpassed 39 million, according to the Johns Hopkins University Coronavirus Resource Center (Center for Systems Science and Engineering, 2021).

2   By the fall of 2020, 57.4 million Americans had filed for unemployment, according to *Forbes* (Kelly, 2020), and over a million people were filing each week at that point, a pace that would have brought total unemployment claims for the year to over 80 million.

3   Big Brother is a fictional character and symbol in George Orwell's dystopian novel *1984*. He is ostensibly the leader of Oceania, a totalitarian state, wherein the ruling party wields total power over the citizens.

misbehavior by mask wearers and mask haters. But, ironically, the most egregious misbehaving, from a behavioral perspective, came from the government. Decision makers forgot everything about choice architecture and tried to force people to do things a certain way. And when forced or pushed, we naturally push back, even if it is for our own good.

Designing a successful retirement plan involves flirting with this idea of paternalism but doing it in a way that is not heavy-handed, that does not push or coerce, because 401(k) architecture is assisted by "choice architecture" that encourages good decisions without taking away anyone's individual choices.

The key to designing a successful plan is establishing defaults that help rather than harm, keeping the design simple, and overcommunicating. Unnecessary complexity undermines greater engagement, and poor plan design pushes employees too much or pushes them away.

Behavioral Economist Richard Thaler grappled with this issue when designing the Save More Tomorrow program with Shlomo Benartzi.[4] He learned that "paternalism" is a profane word.

---

4 "Save More Tomorrow" refers to both the program utilizing auto-features and behavioral research to improve retirement plan outcomes and the book by the same name: *Save More Tomorrow: Practical Behavioral Finance Solutions to Improve 401(k) Plans* (Benartzi, 2012).

"At the University of Chicago, you can call someone a Marxist, an anarchist, or even a Green Bay Packers fan (the archrival of the Chicago Bears, the local NFL team), but calling a colleague a paternalist is the cruelest cut of all... Normally we think that paternalism involves coercion, as when people are required to contribute to Social Security or forbidden to buy alcohol or drugs [or forced to wear masks]. But Save More Tomorrow is a voluntary program...Maybe we should call it, I don't know, libertarian paternalism."[5]

Every workplace retirement plan has a default setting. The default is simply what happens if an employee does not do something. The defaults should be set up to encourage employees toward behavior they might otherwise self-select when thinking and acting reasonably. But the defaults must not push them toward this behavior (or they might push back) and must allow them to override those choices. This is the art of choice architecture.

In bowling, for example, the objective is to keep the ball out of the gutter and to strike the pins. Bumpers that prevent the ball from landing in the gutter are an aid but may be perceived as a hindrance, even if they help the ball to stay out of the gutter, moving in the direction the bowler intended. This is the balancing act with proper plan design: to encourage but not to coerce.

---

[5] *Misbehaving: The Making of Behavioral Economics*, Richard Thaler, 2015. P. 322.

DESIGNING DEFAULTS THAT HELP RATHER THAN HARM

At the risk of appearing too paternalistic, some employers try to avoid setting plan defaults. But it is fundamentally impossible to avoid defaults. A plan default is simply what happens in the absence of an election, and every plan has them, so set your defaults to meet the goals of the plan.

Auto-features, for example, automatically enroll employees who do not make an election (defaulting them into the plan unless they specifically opt out) and automatically increase contributions if they do not opt out of increases. The absence of intentional auto-features means employees are automatically *not* enrolled if they do not make an election (defaulting them out of the plan unless they specifically opt in). In either scenario, there is still a default, and the employees are still automatically impacted; the difference is whether it requires an opt-out or an opt-in to reverse being swept in or left out.

The goal of the 401(k) is to help your employees save, so a well-designed plan uses auto-enrollment to set defaults that help. Popularized by Save More Tomorrow, it has increasingly become commonplace, particularly for mid- to large-sized employers. In fact, it is uncommon today for large retirement plans to not use auto-enrollment, and it is growing in popularity among small employers.

Default investments are also an important feature in plan design, particularly for plans using auto-enrollment. If employees are enrolled in a plan without an investment election, a fund must be designated (by default) to receive those contributions. When 401(k) plans were first established, defaulted contributions were rare, and the default fund was generally the cash account. The Pension Protection Act of 2006 provided safe harbor protection for employers adopting the auto-features, allowing you to default your employees into a default investment that provided additional protection—a Qualified Default Investment Alternative (QDIA).

The QDIA must be an appropriately diversified portfolio that would not be harmful if the plan participant never moved their money out after being defaulted. For this reason, the QDIA may not be cash (or a cash equivalent like a money market or stable value fund) because cash is not appropriate for long-term investing (and most employees defaulted into a fund remain in that fund rather than reallocating or rediversifying their account).

Typically, the QDIA is a Target Date Fund (an age-based portfolio), though it may be a risk-based portfolio. Or sometimes the QDIA is a Managed Accounts program, although this is not an advisable practice. If your employees are defaulted to a portfolio, like Managed Accounts, that costs more than other investments, it places you as the plan fiduciary at tremendous risk. Managed Accounts should only be used as the QDIA if they are offered at no additional cost.

And so the ubiquitous Target Date Fund remains the most prevalent QDIA on the market, although custom Target Date Fund portfolios are gaining in popularity as a more sophisticated option.

TARGET DATE FUNDS AS THE QDIA

As plans increasingly adopt auto-enrollment features using Target Date Funds (TDFs) as the default investment, most money in workplace retirement plans is held in TDFs. Unfortunately, TDFs are not understood thoroughly or scrutinized adequately.

WHAT IS A TARGET DATE FUND?

The TDF is intended to be an investor's single retirement asset, like one-stop shopping. It is a portfolio diversified between different asset classes (stocks, bonds, cash) that shifts the allocation (and the commensurate risk) as a plan participant nears retirement. For example, if a person will be at or near retirement in 2040, selecting a 2040 Target Date Fund diversifies their investments in a prudent manner for someone their age. As they get closer to the year 2040, the management team of the TDF pulls back on the throttle (the investment in stocks) to protect the accumulated wealth and to hedge against a drop in the market at the end of the journey, when it would be most catastrophic. TDFs are built on the idea that young investors can afford to be more aggressive, while older investors may want to be more conservative.

The power of TDFs is broad diversification, automatically rebalancing over the years, and shifting risk allocation. The shift is crucial because many employees never revisit their original allocation. (This is also why age-based allocations are better than risk-based allocations. A person's risk may shift over time, but the risk-based portfolio is static, whereas an age-based portfolio would have gradually shifted in risk.) TDFs work for those who truly want to *set it and forget it*. My experience is that most employees appreciate the one-stop shopping, they want a guided portfolio to do it for them, and 90% to 95% use the TDFs. The professional guidance helps inexperienced or less sophisticated investors, it helps us stay disciplined in a long-term strategy rather than market timing, and it protects the employee and employer from unnecessary risk-taking in the market.

HOW ARE TARGET DATE FUNDS MISUNDERSTOOD?

The path of diminishing stock or equity is referred to as a "glidepath" (picture a downward slope as the portfolio transfers risk from 100% stocks to 90% to 80% to 70% and so on). Every TDF has a different glidepath; no two portfolios are built the same. So, to be fair, TDFs are complex instruments, nearly impossible to benchmark or compare. Some glidepaths decrease the number of stocks or equity to age 65 (leveling off thereafter), while others decrease the amount of equity exposure through the target date and into retirement, not reaching the most conservative allocation until age 70 or 75 or even 80. (In the industry, these are called "to" versus "through" strategies.) Some glidepaths decrease the amount of equity to 45%, others to 35%, and others to 25%. This is called the equity landing. Some glidepaths are static, decreasing equity allocations regardless of market conditions, while others are dynamic, taking economic factors into consideration in an actively managed solution. Few people understand the TDFs in their own retirement plan or the type of glidepath in their portfolio. And very few employers conducted a Glidepath Optimization Analysis™ to pick the best glidepath for their unique employee population.

One example of this confusion is a recent Vanguard report that revealed 50% of their 401(k) participants invested in a single TDF, while nearly as many were invested in multiple TDFs or some combination of TDFs and other investments in the core fund lineup. Meant to be a one-stop solution, many investors do not use TDFs correctly. An employee retiring in 2045 should invest 100% of their contributions in the 2045 fund, not 30% in the 2045 fund and 30% in the 2040 fund and 20% in an additional small-cap fund and 20% in the real estate fund.

Another example of the confusion is the employee who believes that because they are in the 2015 fund and it is the year 2020, they are 100% cash (completely out of the market). Depending on their TDF, they might still have a third or half of their money in the market, even after the target year of their portfolio. Employees have generally not received the education to make good choices, while employers have not received the guidance from a plan fiduciary advisor in the selection of their glidepath.

HOW ARE TARGET DATE FUNDS UNDERSCRUTINIZED?

TDFs do not receive proper scrutiny due to the complexity and ensuing confusion and due to the proprietary nature of TDFs sponsored by the Recordkeeper. And the lack of scrutiny is in direct violation of guidance from the Department of Labor. The complexity makes it nearly impossible to compare and evaluate various years from one TDF to another. (Benchmarking the 2045 fund in one series against the 2045 fund from another TDF series is not an apples-to-apples comparison.) And if the TDF is sponsored by the Recordkeeper (using Fidelity Target Date Funds within a plan recordkept by Fidelity, for example),[6] it makes their replacement challenging. And yet, the DOL issued guidance in 2013 about the additional scrutiny we should give TDFs...guidance that has largely been ignored by plan fiduciaries and their plan fiduciary advisors.

Think of it this way. If 90% of retirement plan assets are held in TDFs, and only 10% are held in core funds, the TDFs should receive even more scrutiny. Instead, the core funds receive attention, but TDFs are ignored, partially due to what I call "proprietary handcuffs."

Other providers have learned this trick too. For example, internet and cable providers offer a *free* email address tied to their services, making it difficult to cancel (and making the business "sticky" for them). I learned this years ago when we switched internet providers and established email addresses with the new provider's domain. When we considered switching providers a few years later, we stayed because we did not want to lose the email address tied to that provider (the one we had given friends and family and the school). We stayed with a service provider much longer than we should have stayed, accepting poor service and increased rates, because we were tied to an email address.

---

6   This is not a recommendation, an endorsement, or a criticism of the Target Date Funds from Fidelity, also known as the Fidelity Freedom Funds. This is merely an example for illustration purposes.

When we finally switched, we established emails that could be used on any platform.

With 401(k) plans, if you evaluate the TDFs (as required) and find them deficient, you may feel trapped—tied to the TDFs with proprietary handcuffs because they are sponsored by the Recordkeeper. If your Recordkeeper is JPMorgan, for example, it may seem pointless to place your JPMorgan TDFs on the Watch List. If your Recordkeeper is T. Rowe Price, it may be impossible (or expensive) to remove the T. Rowe Price TDFs and stay at T. Rowe Price for recordkeeping.[7] The proprietary handcuffs discourage some Retirement Plan Committees from their responsibility to monitor funds, ignoring questions about performance because the answers might require moving the entire plan.

The DOL guidelines, however, require scrutiny regardless of how uncomfortable or confusing. And it is confusing— even to the DOL. Shortly after the TDF Tips were released in 2013, I was a presenter at a conference, sharing the stage with a Field Investigator from the DOL, outlining the new guidance. After our presentation, an audience member asked, "Should we use a Target Date Fund that is 'to' or 'through' for our plan?" There are, by the way, two correct answers to this question that the person from the DOL

---

7   This is *not* a recommendation, an endorsement, or a criticism of the Target Date Funds from JPMorgan or the Target Date Funds from T. Rowe Price. This is merely an example for illustration purposes.

could have provided, but he chose neither option.[8] Instead, speaking out of his ignorance rather than on behalf of the DOL, he actually recommended that they should have one of both! Can you imagine how confusing that would be, to offer two different Target Date Funds, a "to" strategy and a "through" strategy, to let employees pick which 2045 fund they want? The DOL agent was confused, and his advice created more confusion.

TDFs are confusing, even to regulators (or at least to this one).

Target Date Funds play an important role in designing defaults that help rather than harm, particularly in finding a default investment that fits for the QDIA, but they should be the most heavily scrutinized and evaluated funds in the plan, and employers should be careful to not just accept the TDF their Recordkeeper gives them.

KEEPING THE DESIGN SIMPLE

As noted above, some of the financial instruments used within the workplace retirement plan (like the Target Date Funds) are complex. But there is tremendous value

---

[8] The best answer would have been "Conduct a Glidepath Optimization Analysis™ to identify which TDF fits best," but the answer I expected was "At the DOL, we're not able to recommend one strategy over the other any more than we can recommend one TDF over another. Each employer should determine this for themselves, maybe with the help of your advisor or other service providers." At least this second response (to not endorse either strategy) is acceptable. Instead, he gave the wrong response: to employ both strategies.

in keeping the plan, the plan investments, and the various features of the plan as simple as possible. More employees participate, more employees save more money, and more employees invest correctly when the plan is easily understood. Unnecessary complexity adds confusion, not confidence, and almost always produces unfavorable results.

The only purpose in adopting layers of intricacies is if that complexity somehow leads to greater simplicity. Case in point: a TDF is complex, but TDFs are used for simple, one-stop shopping. They are complex financial instruments used to simplify the fund choices for plan participants.

Ultimately, in plan design, less is more, and simple is best. As they say in the Navy,[9] "keep it simple, stupid." This KISS principle follows the idea that most things work better if they are kept simple, meaning simplicity should be a key goal in design, and unnecessary complexity should be avoided. As Albert Einstein said, "If you can't explain it simply, you don't understand it well enough."

One of the easiest ways to demonstrate "more is less" in 401(k) plans is with the number of fund options. Multi-

---

9 The KISS acronym may predate the US Navy and may predate this historical reference, but "Project KISS" was referenced in December 1960 by Rear Admiral Paul D. Stroop in the *Chicago Daily Tribune*, so by this time it was a term familiar in the Navy.

ple studies, dating back to the original DALBAR[10] study, continue to find an optimum number of fund choices to maximize results (and, conversely, a threshold of too many fund choices that negatively impacts participation). And the optimum number is much smaller than the average number of funds in most plans.

Employees need to have enough fund options to allow for broad diversification and ERISA 404(c) safe harbor protection.[11] But the number of investments needed to properly diversify your account is not large—maybe only 10 to 15 funds. In fact, plans that offer 20 or more funds have less participation and lower savings rates.[12] The more choices, the more overwhelming and confusing, and the lower the engagement. There is an inverse relationship between the number of funds and participation.

Ironically, there is also an inverse relationship between the number of funds and the size of the plan. Bigger plans often have fewer fund options, while small retirement plans

---

10 DALBAR is a research firm. It is the financial community's leading independent expert for evaluating, auditing, and rating business practices, customer performance, product quality, and service.

11 ERISA section 404(c) is a powerful tool for mitigating fiduciary liability. While 404(c) does not protect plan fiduciaries from making imprudent investment choices at the plan level, it does provide protection when plan participants select investments for their personal account and lose money. In other words, if the plan allows for adequate diversification and qualifies under section 404(c) (and the employees were notified of this arrangement) and an employee still selects not to diversify their money but puts all their money into one fund option that drops in value, the employer is not liable for those losses.

12 According to DALBAR.

offer 30, 50, sometimes as many as 80 or more investment choices. It seems counterintuitive that fewer funds are needed to invest more money. I think it is because larger, more sophisticated plans understand the power of simplicity. The plans I have served that were more than $1 billion often had just six to 10 funds, while we have taken over plans under $10 million that used 100 funds (or more). The reason this inverse relationship is perpetuated is because small plans are often handled by nonspecialists (not a 401k architect but a financial advisor unfamiliar with choice architecture).

The best plan design (in keeping with the law of parsimony) gives employees just two options: the option for professional management and the option to self-direct, listed in that order. And the first option uses either a Target Date Fund or a custom target age portfolio (as the QDIA), while the second option offers a dozen core funds for those self-directing. Adhere to the KISS principle.

In fact, Retirement Plan Committees generally get themselves into trouble when they diverge from simplicity. One committee, for example, was talked into adopting the Fairholme Fund (by an inexperienced advisor). No one on the committee was familiar with Fairholme—it was not the boring, vanilla flavor—but they thought diverging from average or mediocre would produce better-than-average results. In 2010, the fund ranked in the top percentile, but it was too aggressive for a large-cap value position in a 401(k) plan. Within one year, the fund had dropped from first to worst, the absolute worst fund in its category in 2011, and the committee had it on the Watch List. (Their Investment Policy Statement indicated it should have been removed, but, in violation of the IPS, they kept it in the plan and on watch.) A decade later, Morningstar had it rated as a one-star fund with an investment style of small growth rather than large value. Over the last three-, five-, and 10-year periods, Fairholme performed in the 89th, 95th, and 100th percentile.[13] That's right: 100th percentile. In other words, over the last 10 years, it was outperformed by every other fund in its category. The committee had an opportunity to go with slow and steady (and boring), but they took a risk on an unknown entity, and they made that bet with their employees' money! Just keep it simple. And communicate.

COMMUNICATE. COMMUNICATE. COMMUNICATE.

Keep it simple. Communicate, educate, and overcommunicate. Part of the simplicity is how well the employees understand the plan and their options. If the design is simple, but the directions or roadmap is written in a foreign language, it misses the goal. Simple plan design is undergirded and facilitated by great communication.

---

13   The Fairholme Fund (FAIRX) had a three-, five-, and 10-year return of –5.55 (89th percentile), –2.21 (95th percentile), and 1.67 (100th percentile ranking) as of March 31, 2020.

If you are a plan fiduciary, you have two overarching fiduciary responsibilities: the duty to monitor and the duty to educate. Conversely, the value of a plan fiduciary advisor is to facilitate these same two charges. Your 401(k) architect understands plan design and plan investments, and they communicate the plan provisions in common language for you and for your employees.

The better the communication, the simpler the plan, and the higher the employee morale, the better the employee engagement.

Simplicity keeps the plan on track and produces better results.

PLAN DESIGN 101

USING GOALS-BASED ARCHITECTURE TO ADD PLAN FEATURES

The goal in designing a 401(k) that serves your purpose and your people is to help more employees save more money, to help every employee cross the finish line, and to leave no employee behind. Purpose-driven plan design uses *goals-based architecture*: only adopting plan design features that support plan goals.

Every plan design decision should pass through the filter of "What would a healthy plan do?" (WWHPD).

Thinking about adding loans to the 401(k) plan? Or adding a second or third loan option?

What would a healthy plan do? Are more loans going to help more people save more money, producing healthier outcomes that get more people across the finish line? (Probably not!)

You are bound, as a plan fiduciary, by the fiduciary standard to always do what is exclusively in the best interest of plan participants, not what benefits the company or the 401(k) plan. But plan design is considered an administrative decision or a "settlor function," held to a lesser standard. One example is the employer match. Implementing (or raising) the match is always in the best interest of your employees but may not be in your best interest. (It faces the tension between people and profits or purpose and profits.)

But purpose-driven businesses hold plan design to an even higher standard, choosing goals-based architecture for putting money into the plan, growing money within the plan, and taking money out of the plan.

With every plan feature, ask, "What would a healthy plan do?"

HEALTHY FEATURES THAT IMPACT PUTTING MONEY INTO THE PLAN

Goals-based architecture is related to choice architecture: designing choices and options that produce beneficial outcomes. There are a variety of choices you make about plan design that help employees make better choices about putting money into the plan, putting more money into the plan, and putting the right kind of money into the plan.

The IRS sets the contribution limit for workplace retirement plans and (generally) increases it each year. The limitation is defined under IRS Code Section 402(g)(1). Added to the limit is an additional catch-up contribution for those age 50 and older. The catch-up contribution provision was created by the Economic Growth and Tax Relief Reconciliation Act of 2001 (EGTRRA) to help older employees save more. The original contribution limit in 1978 was $45,475 because the 402(g) limit and 415 limit were combined.[1] In 1982, the contribution limit dropped to $30,000, and then the Tax Reform Act of 1986 segregated the 402(g) and 415 ($7,000 for personal savings and $30,000 for total contributions). And since 1986, the 402(g) limit has increased periodically.

The IRS limits how much we can contribute because every dollar contributed impacts how little we pay in taxes. The 402(g) limit reduces the "tax asylum" to less than $20,000 a year. But contributing as much as one can afford, up to the allowable limit, produces better retirement outcomes, and you should make choices in plan design to help employees maximize these contribution limits.

---

1   The 402(g) limit is how much an employee can contribute. The 415 limit is the total of how much can be contributed by the employee and by the employer on behalf of the employee.

I am periodically surprised to find 401(k) plans that still allow less than 100% in contributions. The correct plan design allows employee contributions of 100%, up to the maximum allowed under 402(g).[2] But while the 402(g) threshold is a dollar limit, good plan design only allows contributions as a percentage, not a dollar amount, because percentages promote better outcomes.

The employer match, after all, is expressed in a percentage, so employee contributions conveyed by a similar measurement are complementary. Second, studies show that employees save more when their contributions are stated as a percentage rather than a dollar amount, and getting more people to save more money is the goal. And third, framing the proposition as a percentage of current income is helpful when the goal is a percentage of income replacement.

Companies that still allow employees to contribute a dollar amount have an education gap with connecting employee money to the company match. If the company is matching, for example, 50% of 5%, an employee contribution of 5% makes sense, but an employee contribution of $50 does not. The goal is to maximize the match, so setting contributions at 5% ensures no free money is left on the table. Plan design that only allows for percentages facilitates more employees hitting the match.

---

2   It is possible, in some cases, that a person joining the 401(k) late in the year would need to contribute 100% to hit the maximum contribution limit before year-end.

Furthermore, employees save more when contributions are expressed in percentages rather than dollars. Behavioral Finance calls this concept "mental accounting": the tendency of people to develop and make decisions based on purely mental categories. For example, if 6% of my paycheck is $100, a contribution of 6% and a contribution of $100 should be viewed identically. Instead, a person feels greater pain if contributing $100 because they imagine other things $100 might have purchased. (It is much harder in mental accounting to think of other things 6% might have purchased.) Handing over $100 in cold, hard cash hurts more, and loss aversion (another principle from Behavioral Finance) is real. We do not like to be separated from our money. But in mental accounting, we value a percentage differently; we put it in a different "bucket" in our mind. Being separated from 6% of our paycheck is considerably less painful than being separated from $100. And receiving 94% of our paycheck (with 6% deposited in our 401k before we see it) is practically pain-free.

Furthermore, most people think of dollars in whole numbers, while percentages are unlikely to equate to whole numbers, making dollars harder to increase. One person, for example, starts out saving $50, and *if* they increase the amount, it will be in whole numbers, with each increase exacerbating the pain. It is unlikely, for instance, that they increase from $50 to $52.75. Instead, they will remain at $50 until making the huge, painful leap to $75 and then to

$100, possibly stopping short of an unbearable mark, like $200. Conversely, their colleague saving 5% can increase contributions easily, just 1% at a time, reaching a much larger amount much less painfully, an amount that almost always exceeds contributions in dollars.

The goal is to get more people to save more money, which is easier with percentages than dollar amounts. The ultimate goal is income replacement, helping employees replace 70% (or more) of their income and live on 70% (or less) of their income. I call this the Rule of 70.[3] The dollar amount does not matter. What matters is replacing a percentage of current income, which is easier to do (and easier to explain) when saving a percentage.

My advice is to *only* allow percentages, starting with a high enough percentage to maximize the potential for a successful outcome. Increasingly, 401(k) plans use auto-enrollment, but far too many enroll too low, which limits successful outcomes. If the contribution goal is 15%, starting contributions too low may result in them taking too long to reach 15%. You can enroll your employees at any percentage, but the key is to start high enough to maximize success and low enough to deter unenrollment. Starting them at 3% means very few unenroll, but most can tolerate starting higher. Experience has shown very few employees unen-

---

3 For a full explanation of the Rule of 70, please refer to my previous book, *Repurposement* (Redstone, 2019).

roll when starting auto-enrollment at 5% or even 6% (7% is where some employees start pushing back). Start at the highest palatable number and implement auto-increases to slowly raise contributions. The two biggest mistakes with auto-enrollment are starting employees too low and failing to systematically increase contributions over time. The success of the 401(k) hinges on getting enough money in.

Of course, it also helps to put the right kind of money into the plan. And by this, I mean taking advantage of Roth contributions, which are after-tax contributions that allow tax-free earnings. Good plan design allows Roth, promotes Roth, and allows in-plan Roth conversions. Roth contributions are critical for success.[4]

For example, if an employee contributes $50,000 tax-deferred, and, after four decades, the account has grown to $500,000, the entire time they were contributing, they were postponing taxes. When they retire, however, rather than paying taxes on $50,000, they pay taxes on $500,000 (the amount of their contributions plus earnings). This is not a bad arrangement—paying taxes later is a good arrangement, and having the money increase is good, even if it increases the tax bill—but Roth provides an even better arrangement.

---

4   Some have suggested that the net result is similar if employees take out the taxes first and contribute less, but since both pre-tax and Roth contributions are based on the Gross Amount (before taxes) the resulting contribution amount should be identical. In other words, employees rarely adjust contributions to be less if contributing in Roth, and when Roth contributions are equal, the net result is superior with the tax savings.

If the employee contributes $50,000 in Roth, and, after four decades, the account has grown to $500,000, the entire time they were contributing, they were paying taxes. When they retire, they do *not* owe taxes on $50,000 (it was contributed after tax), nor do they owe taxes on the earnings. They pay no taxes at retirement. It cost them more to build the account over time because they paid the taxes along the way, but their net tax savings is substantially larger.[5]

In the first example, the employee pays taxes on $500,000 (when they take distribution). But in the Roth example, the employee only pays taxes on $50,000 (when they put it in).

Conversely, in the Roth example, they have $500,000 to retire. But in the first example, the employee has less than $500,000 because some of the account belongs to the IRS.

The power of Roth is tax-free earnings—not having to pay any taxes on the increase—so Roth makes sense for employees who have a lot of time left for those earnings to increase. If a person is planning to retire in 10 years or less, it may make more sense to simply defer taxes. But if the money will be invested for decades, the earnings could be substantial, making it worthwhile to pay the taxes up front

---

[5] The fact that it costs more is the primary reason Roth may not make sense. If a person cannot afford to contribute at least the amount necessary to receive the full match, they need to contribute pretax to at least hit the employer match. In other words, they may need to contribute less in taxes so they can afford to contribute more in 401(k) contributions.

and let the account grow tax-free. Roth makes a lot of sense for younger employees.

But Roth also makes sense for employees of any age if they are highly compensated. (Note: You, as the owner, may personally want to contribute in Roth.)[6] The Roth IRA has earnings limits to prevent highly paid employees from benefiting, but earnings limits do not apply to a Roth 401(k) plan. (Earnings limits do not apply to any 401k contributions, pretax or Roth.) Highly compensated employees may have never had the Roth option available to them until joining a company with a Roth 401(k).

A person who earns more and can afford to pay the taxes now benefits from the incredible wealth-building power of Roth. Plus, Roth contributions are not subject to Required Minimum Distributions[7] (RMDs),[8] and Roth allows tax-free money to pass to beneficiaries in estate planning.[9]

---

6   This is not tax advice and I am not a tax advisor. This is just common sense about your dollars and cents. You should always consult your tax advisor about your particular situation, as it may differ. My experience, however, is that when plan participants tell their accountant that they have a Roth option, the CPA almost always tells them to use it. In fact, some accountants even advise using Roth at a much older age than I typically recommend.

7   The required minimum age at which an account holder was required to take distributions was historically the year in which they reached 70½ years of age, but the SECURE Act increased the age to 72.

8   Technically, contributions in the 401(k) are subject to an RMD unless the plan participant is still employed, but contributions in a Roth 401(k) can easily be rolled into a Roth IRA upon retirement, and a Roth IRA is not subject to an RMD.

9   Beneficiaries may still be subject to taking an RMD from a Roth account, although the money is tax-free.

HEALTHY CHOICES THAT IMPACT GROWING MONEY WITHIN THE PLAN

There are a variety of choices you can make to impact the growth of the money within the plan. Good choice architecture addresses how much employees contribute, how much employers contribute, and how closely employees stay the course over time.

A healthy plan addresses how much an employee contributes by utilizing auto-enrollment and auto-escalation to make sure no employee is left behind.

As mentioned previously, every plan should implement automatic enrollment. (Every plan has a default, and the default should be into the plan unless employees opt out of the plan.) And every plan should utilize auto-increases to help account holders replace 70% or more of their income. This is just Plan Design 101. But advanced plan design also uses the employee's age to establish the appropriate defaults. In fact, without benchmarking to a person's age, some auto-features could be counterproductive.

Auto-enrollment works great, for example, if employees work for the same company their entire career. But the Bureau of Labor Statistics reports that the average person holds 11.7 jobs during their lifetime, so if a person switches employers a dozen times, they may have their 401(k) contributions reset a dozen times. If the "reset" is not indexed for age, it can be counterproductive. An employee auto-enrolled at 5% and auto-increased to 15% works great if they stay long enough to reach 15% or if their next company does not auto-enroll and roll them back to 5%. In other words, if an employee switches jobs and each employer resets the savings rate to 5%, a tool meant to help could actually cause harm.

The employee has the option of overriding the auto-features, of course, but they may not; the typical plan participant stays where they are auto-enrolled. Therefore, older employees should be auto-enrolled at a higher percentage. They can choose to change the percentage, but indexing the default percentage ensures fewer employees are left behind.

A healthy plan also addresses how much the employer contributes, set at a level to maximize employee contributions.

Adopting a Safe Harbor match, for example, allows highly compensated employees to maximize savings. Without a Safe Harbor match, some plan participants may receive refunds.[10]

---

[10] If a plan fails the required discrimination testing when comparing the contribution and deferral ratios between highly compensated employees and non-highly compensated employees, the highly compensated employees may have to take back a refund of some of their contributions. In other words, they overcontributed (not based on the 402g limit but based on how much more they contributed as compared to the rest of the employees)...and the plan is deemed discriminatory in the favor of the highly compensated.

Or if a Safe Harbor match is not in the company budget, there is still a way to be smart with the match. If the company can only contribute 2%, for example, a better design is 50% of 4% or even 25% of 8% rather than 100% of 2%. This encourages employees to save more to get the match.

A healthy plan also addresses how closely employees stay the course. The key to success is purposeful consistency, a faithful and sustained movement in the right direction. Good plan design focuses less on the speed of that movement than on preventing divergence from that course. Even a conservative portfolio can produce higher returns and better results than an aggressive portfolio mixed with market timing. In other words, the employee who chooses the slow-growth path might finish first, while the employee who chooses the fast-growth path finishes second if they take too many detours. Remember the fable of the tortoise and the hare. Your 401(k) architect can design a plan to encourage employees to stay the course, to avoid self-directing and market timing, and to stick with it regardless of market conditions.

Brokerage accounts inside a 401(k), for example, encourage "meddling" rather than the hands-off consistency needed to see results over a long period of time. The 401(k) plan should offer just two options: a professionally managed portfolio for most employees and a manageable list of core funds for sophisticated self-directors. Offering a third option, like a brokerage window to "leave" the plan and invest in individual stocks, is not smart.

Keep in mind that purpose-driven plan design focuses on the goal of discouraging self-directing and encouraging employees to stay the course. I believe offering a brokerage window increases your liability (offering access to investments the RPC will not monitor) while encouraging self-directing. The very existence of a brokerage window encourages day trading and market timing. Employees are welcome to do day trading and market timing—outside the plan—in an outside brokerage account. The 401(k) plan is not a brokerage account.

The 401(k) plan should be designed to encourage employees to stick with it through turbulent market cycles. If an employee is in the appropriate portfolio, they will stay the course; if they are in the wrong portfolio (more aggressive than they can stomach), they try to get out of the roller coaster midflight, and that's when people get hurt.

Market timing is a strategy of buying or selling based on predictions of future market conditions. But no one knows the future, not even the professionals. And without a crystal ball, it is a very expensive guess.

Fidelity conducted a study of the impact of market timing over four decades and found that missing out on just the five best days in the market dropped overall return by 35%, while missing out on the 10 best days in the market dropped overall return in half! A 40-year time period is roughly 10,000 days of stock trading. Market timing means a person is betting they can get in and out of the market at the right time and not miss out on one of those 10 days. It works much better to just stay invested rather than risk timing it incorrectly.

The Center for Retirement Research at Boston College examined the impact of market timing on professional managers by comparing TDF managers that do not diverge from their glidepath with those TDF managers that do diverge from the glidepath when they believe there is an opportunity to time the market. The study is fascinating because it only focused on professional managers, and it only looked at TDF strategies, easily benchmarked with their established glidepaths. The differences were statistically significant. Those who tried to time the market had performance returns that lagged the others by 14.1 basis points a year (0.141 percentage points), which compounds over the lifetime of the average investor. And these are the pros! The adverse impact of market timing for the rest of us is much more profound.

Helping employees stick to their plan, by the way, is one of the reasons TDFs are so effective. In a TDF, the gradual reduction in riskier assets, known as the glidepath, keeps participants on track. As employees get closer to retirement, two things happen, both of which impact their risk tolerance. First, as their time frame shortens, they become less capable of recovering from drops in the market. And second, as their account balance increases, they become more risk-averse with more at stake. Losing a third of their account when they had $1,000 was less painful, but losing a third of their account when they have $100,000 or $1 million is catastrophic. As age and balances increase, the typical person becomes increasingly risk-averse (because they become increasingly loss-averse). In fact, the average person who is months or even weeks away from retirement may be hyper-risk-averse. They become what I call a Will Rogers investor: "More concerned with the return *of* my money than the return *on* my money."[11] [emphasis added]

HEALTHY CHOICES THAT IMPACT TAKING MONEY OUT OF THE PLAN

Goals-based design adds plan features by considering what gets the most money *into* the plan and what *keeps* the most money in the plan. Avoiding preretirement distributions is important to building wealth, but it is not as simple as saying preretirement distributions are always wrong. The three tips about preretirement distributions include a green light, a caution light, and a red light: say yes (almost always)

---

[11] A quote from Will Rogers, the actor and humorist from the early 20th century, as quoted in *Will Rogers, Performer*, 292.

to hardship distributions, be cautious about in-service distributions, and say no (almost always) to loans.

Employees are encouraged to think of the 401(k) as a long-term retirement savings plan, not a short-term solution for cash flow problems. And yet, there are times when undue financial hardships create a real burden. In the 401(k) world, "hardship" is not defined by the employee but by the IRS. There are very specific purposes for allowing hardships that must be documented and approved, and under these circumstances, it is permissible and advisable to allow hardship distributions. A 401(k) plan design that does not allow hardships may hurt participation and may appear insensitive. And since the IRS regulates the parameters, it is not exactly like opening a floodgate for everyone to take their money. You should (generally) allow hardships.

My advice is to work with a service provider (preferably an Administrative Fiduciary) who takes responsibility for the approval process. This shifts the burden to the provider for documentation (since documentation is key in the event of an audit), but it also shifts the approval process away from the company (in case the documentation does not support the claim and must be denied).

For example, one of the IRS-approved reasons for hardship is to maintain your shelter. If a person is facing eviction from their apartment or foreclosure on their house, a hardship distribution can prevent them from being homeless if the employee submits a copy of their eviction notice or the foreclosure notice. If a person is behind on their rent but has not received an eviction notice yet, it may be a financial hardship for the employee, but it is not a hardship from the IRS perspective. Allowing hardship distributions for real emergencies is wise, but emphasize break-the-glass emergencies only, use tight guidelines to stem the tide of distributions, and let your 3(16) administrator manage the approval process.

Allowing hardship distributions is *almost* always a greenlight situation, although we had an example just this year when it might not have made sense. The CARES Act[12] allowed Coronavirus-Related Distributions (CRDs) of 100% of a person's account balance up to $100,000 if the plan participant or any of their dependents were adversely impacted by the pandemic. When Congress rushed to implement this provision, they opened the door to a mass exodus in the 401(k) industry, a mistake for which American workers may be paying for many years. One of the mistakes of the CRDs, unlike the typical hardship, is that the burden of proof is on the employee; the approval process is undocumented, unmanaged by service providers, and easily manipulated to gain preretirement distributions.

---

12   The Coronavirus Aid, Relief, and Economic Security (CARES) Act was passed by Congress with overwhelming bipartisan support, pumping trillions of dollars into the US economy in the largest stimulus bill in history.

Furthermore, very few Americans needed $100,000, at least not at one time. According to the Bureau of Labor Statistics, the median income for Americans at the end of 2019 was $48,672. The pandemic was disruptive, but it seems unlikely that the average American worker needed a distribution that was twice their annual salary.

Some service providers rushed to implement CRDs, even using an opt-out approval process of putting the provision in every 401(k) plan unless the Plan Sponsors opted out.[13] We coached plan participants through our toll-free number to *slow the flow* if seeking a CRD. After all, the CARES Act did not restrict the number of CRDs, so our message continued to be "Just take what you absolutely need to get you through the next few weeks, and if you need more after that, call us back." Unfortunately, not every company or every advisor took this approach, and some employees emptied their accounts. The pandemic was catastrophic, but because of the CARES Act, it may prove to be catastrophic years from now as retirement is delayed for decades. CRDs are a great example of when not to green-light every hardship.

Plan fiduciaries can (almost always) say yes to hardship withdrawals but should generally be more cautious with in-service withdrawals.

---

13   This was a mistake because the default option should have been the option consistent with a goals-based design of keeping more money in the plan. The default should have been to opt in if the Plan Sponsor believed their employees needed this provision rather than an opt-out.

Typically, distribution from a 401(k) plan is available at retirement or upon separation from the company (even if prior to retirement age) or under the conditions of a hardship, as previously described, or in the event of death or disability. In some cases, however, plans also allow in-service distributions at 59½ years of age, even if the employee is still on payroll. The age factor is important because withdrawals at age 59½ avoid an additional 10% tax penalty for an early distribution, but that does not mean early distributions are beneficial for employees, and, in fact, they could be harmful. You do not have to allow in-service withdrawals at 59½ and may want to proceed with caution if considering this option.

The general rule of thumb is that your money should be where your feet are, so if you leave a company for a job elsewhere, roll the money forward to the next company's 401(k). If you move again, move the money again, and keep rolling it forward so the money is working wherever you are working. The only reason not to roll it forward is if your new company does not offer a 401(k) plan.

Rolling the money out of the workplace retirement account into an Individual Retirement Account (an IRA) is almost always a mistake, will generally cost more in investment fees, and only makes sense to the financial advisor who profits from *capturing* the rollover.

If an employee is still in service (still employed), they should not be taking a withdrawal. In-service withdrawals were a concession to the insurance industry and do not facilitate building wealth for retirement. In fact, some financial advisors show up at a company with a list of everyone over 59½ to capture rollovers, sometimes into an expensive annuity. I have had some clients remove this feature from their plan because local advisors were using fearmongering to take advantage of their employees. Employers should proceed with caution on allowing in-service distributions, noting that it is not a required provision.

Plan fiduciaries may also want to say no to loan options in the plan, although it is not a simple no in every situation. Generally, it is best if the plan does not allow loans because preretirement distributions are harmful to building wealth. The exception to the rule is if a plan is experiencing extremely low participation, and, as a last-ditch effort, giving employees preretirement access to their money incentivizes more to invest. My advice is to avoid this step at all costs, and only as a last resort acquiesce to the loan provision. (Note that once the provision is in the plan, it is difficult to remove.) And never, under any circumstance, allow more than one loan. The 401(k) that allows employees to take multiple loans is enabling poor money management, inviting them to use the investments for current cash flow rather than retirement.

Proponents of loans will argue it is better to borrow the

money from yourself than from a bank, but it is far better to budget and practice good stewardship. Other proponents will argue the interest paid makes up for the harm of removing the money from the market, but since you are paying yourself the interest, money paid to yourself is a net-zero return, or revenue-neutral. And the double taxation consequences of a loan are harmful. The loans are repaid in after-tax dollars that are then taxed again upon distribution or, if unpaid (in the event of a loan default), the loan is immediately taxable and (if the employee is under 59½) incurs the additional 10% tax penalty.

When plan fiduciaries are considering loans, they should see a red light (in most cases).

The biggest obstacle to building a healthy retirement plan is losing sight of the goal when designing the plan. The primary goal is to get as many people across the finish line as possible. Your goal in offering a plan is to attract and retain great employees, but, ultimately, the goal is to help retire loyal employees.

And while plan design is a settlor function (not a fiduciary function) the burden for those who want to build healthy plans is to still do what is in the best interest of plan participants: to prioritize plan features that put more money into the plan, grow money within the plan, and keep money in the plan.

Ask yourself, "What would a healthy plan do?"

FINANCIAL WELLNESS

HEALTHY 401(K) PLANS WORK BEST IN HEALTHY CULTURES

It is hard to build a great home in a shaky location or lay a solid foundation on shaky ground. To design a great 401(k) that serves your purpose and your people, 401(k) architecture should address the larger company context and culture and build the retirement plan within the framework of a holistic wellness program.

It is not impossible to build on shaky ground, but it is hard and very expensive. My brother purchased some great land on the side of a hill in Tennessee to build his home but had to spend more on shoring up the foundation than most people spend on their house.

A healthy retirement plan does best inside the context of a healthy culture, a company culture that balances purpose and profits and people, and a business striving to be a good corporate citizen. If the culture is sick, it will be revealed eventually.

Many people were sick in 2020, not just the millions of confirmed cases during the COVID-19 pandemic, but millions of others who were asymptomatic.

Similarly, workplace retirement plans are asymptomatic—the plans are sick but are not showing signs—or presymptomatic—because the plans are not showing signs *yet*. A 401(k) is healthy if it produces healthy retirement outcomes. (You will know them by their fruits.[1]) The problem with sick plans is that the sickness may not be discovered for many years, sometimes not until it is too late. To avoid building for decades on a shaky foundation, set yourself up for success by constructing the 401(k) inside of a holistic financial wellness program. The goal is *Retirement Readiness*, and being ready to retire involves more than just saving money in the 401(k).

---

[1] Matthew 7:16 NKJV

RETIREMENT READINESS

The term "Retirement Readiness" references how prepared an employee is to cross the finish line, or the degree to which they are on target to reach their eventual goal of income replacement to maintain the same standard of living.

I define Retirement Readiness by the "Rule of 70." It is *the ability to replace 70% or more of your income and to live on 70% or less of your income.* Some may recommend higher income replacement. My recommendation of 70% is because (a) it is an attainable goal, and (b) it is the line of demarcation for success. Replacing 70% (or more) means experiencing a similar lifestyle in retirement.

To replace more is fine. But replacing less than 70% of our income will almost certainly mean an adjustment in lifestyle.

Another reason 70% works well is because Social Security replaces about a third of what the average retiree needs.[2] Admittedly, while Social Security checks are not growing larger, they still supplement a portion, making it *unnecessary* for many of us to replace 100% of our income with our own savings.

---

[2] Income replacement is about one-third on average but varies widely depending on household income. According to the "Guide to Retirement," 2020 edition, p. 15, a household earning $30,000 has 60% of income replacement from Social Security, a household earning $100,000 has 38%, and a household earning $300,000 has 12%.

But the Rule of 70 is not just the ability to replace 70% or more of income; it is also the ability to live on 70% or less of our income.

Employees struggling to live within their means now (living on less than 100%) may struggle with the idea of living on 70% (or less) in retirement. Replacing 70% (or more) means being a good steward. Living on 70% (or less) means retiring debt-free. And both stewardship and debt-free living are essential to success.

How can one replace 70% of their income? By living on less than they make and investing some for the future. If employees live on 100% of what they make, it does not work. And many Americans live on more than 100% of what they make, using plastic rather than cash.

If we cannot learn to live within our means during the working years, we have little chance of successfully navigating life when the income drops. And the average American has 24% of their paycheck going toward consumer debt![3] Founding Father Patrick Henry is best known for his declaration in 1775: "Give me liberty or give me death!" But 245 years later, the country he helped found has spurned financial freedom to cry, "Keep the liberty. Give me debt!"

Based on the debt-to-income (DTI) ratio, we are not a finan-

---
3   US Census Bureau, 2014.

cially healthy society. The recommended DTI for lenders is no more than 28%. But the maximum allowable DTI to still qualify for a mortgage is 43%. In other words, the banking industry thinks 28% debt is healthy, but some lenders will increase our debt up to 43%!

I recommend DTI should be 0% when we reach retirement, and the sooner we get it to 0%, the sooner we can cross the finish line.

According to the US Census Bureau, the median household income is increasing, but the average household debt is increasing by a larger margin. We must learn to live within our means, which may mean tightening the budget. Dave Ramsey says, "I've got good news and bad news. The bad news is you're going to have to tighten your belt and reduce your spending, but the good news is you get to choose when." We can make some tough choices now, getting our money under control now, when it is our choice, or we will have to later, when we do not have a choice.

At one extreme is the person who lives beyond their means and has a huge reduction in lifestyle later. At the other extreme is the person who lives like a pauper to fund a fabulous lifestyle later (which could work if they live long enough to enjoy the rewards of so much sacrifice). But I recommend having a manageable lifestyle now to fund a similar income in retirement.

And the sooner we adopt a healthy lifestyle, the sooner we can cross the finish line into a healthy retirement. Well-being is the key.

THE WELLNESS MOVEMENT

Bill Hettler, MD, is the father of the wellness movement. In 1969, he began promoting the importance of wellness to overall health. He also emphasized the connection between lifestyle choices and wellness, believing good behavior facilitated health.

In 1976, he introduced "The Six Dimensions of Wellness":

1. Physical
2. Social
3. Intellectual
4. Spiritual
5. Emotional
6. Occupational

In 1977, he helped start the National Wellness Institute (NWI). In the first few decades, the NWI operated in relative obscurity—they were a really big deal to a very small number of people—but in the last decade, due to the rising cost of healthcare, the wellness movement entered the workplace. Perhaps it is at your workplace.

Many companies have a wellness program that undergirds the healthcare plan. Weight loss initiatives, cessation of smoking programs, and biometric screenings improve the health of employees, but they also improve healthcare costs. Eventually, a more holistic approach incorporated emotional and intellectual wellness, with voluntary benefits like counseling, while spiritual wellness ushered in chaplaincy programs, particularly in high-stress environments like law enforcement.

Financial wellness was even slower to arrive. Today, only 17 states have financial education as a requirement to graduate high school.[4] In 33 states, financial literacy is either an elective or not offered, so schools produce financially illiterate graduates, and those poor money habits are brought into your workplace, exacerbating the need for financial wellness.

Perhaps financial wellness had a slower adoption rate because it was not part of Hettler's initial six dimensions of wellness, or maybe because it was not part of NWI's

---

[4] According to the Council for Economic Education, 22 states require high school students to take a course in economics, but only 17 states require students to take a course in personal finance, and, according to the Financial Report Card from Champlain College's Center for Financial Literacy, only five states received an A for their financial education efforts: Alabama, Virginia, Tennessee, Utah, and Missouri (Is your state making the grade, 2017). Check out how your state rated: champlain.edu/centers-of-experience/center-for-financial-literacy/report-national-high-school-financial-literacy

initiatives for years,[5] or maybe because the correlation between finances and psychology was not understood until the advent of Behavioral Economics in 2002,[6] or maybe because the retirement plan industry tried to solve an unhealthy system with retirement education. Whatever the reason, the ROI of (and need for) financial wellness is clear.

The "experiment" that began in the 1980s struggled as companies shifted responsibility from employer to employee when shifting from "Defined Benefit" pension plans to "Defined Contribution" 401(k) plans. A few decades into this "experiment," we find that too few employees save too little money. The system was broken, and the retirement industry tried to fix it with retirement education, and then with auto-features. But more must be done.

According to a 2016 study by T. Rowe Price, 48% of employees reported they cannot afford to contribute more to their retirement plans. It does not help to tell broke people to just save more!

The problem is not low balances in the 401(k) plan. That

---

[5] As of June 2020, the NWI offers a resource they describe as a "financial wellness tool," but they also offer members "discounts from Quicken Loans," so it seems that the NWI still doesn't understand financial wellness or how it fits into a holistic wellness program.

[6] Behavioral Finance is a new discipline. In 2002, behavioral psychologist Daniel Kahneman won the Nobel Prize in Economics for his seminal work on Behavioral Economics. His work recognized the important role of emotion in decision-making. It had long been speculated that emotions impact our ability to make good decisions, but there was no science behind it prior to Kahneman's work.

is a *symptom* of a problem. The problem is that they have no budget or they do not have a financial plan to increase that low balance.

The problem is not low contribution rates in the 401(k). That too is a *symptom*. The problem is consumer debt that keeps employees from saving more, even if they want to.

The problem is not too many loans from the 401(k). That is a *symptom*. The problem is the lack of an emergency fund, leaving some employees with no choice but to take a 401(k) loan when disaster strikes.

After years of effort and a ton of money, retirement education has largely failed to move the needle on plan health. I think this is because retirement education does not address the root issue.

Companies adopted other wellness initiatives when the ROI was obvious. (A healthy workforce costs less in insurance premiums.) Financial wellness has had a slower adoption rate because the ROI was unclear at first.

The results of financial wellness took longer to manifest, but the results are dramatic and almost always outpace the savings of physical wellness, particularly over time, because an aging workforce unable to retire is much more expensive than paying extra insurance premiums. One poll found that a third of workers put off medical treatment in the last year because of cost (showing a correlation between financial wellness and physical wellness).[7] And financial troubles can decrease productivity in the workplace by as much as 24 hours a month. An aging workforce experiences higher absenteeism, more workers' comp claims (and higher claims), higher disability premiums, and higher healthcare premiums. And the payroll costs of tenured employees is higher, making the cost of an aging workforce much more expensive.

"Broke" has become the new normal, but it does not just impact your employees who are living beyond their means; being broke affects your business. Financial stress compromises their health and happiness as well as their relationships at home and at work. It compromises their productivity today and their ability to retire tomorrow, which is very expensive for your business.

The problem is bigger than just low deferrals and too many 401(k) loans, and the problem will not be fixed with traditional retirement education. In fact, the Recordkeeper will not fix the problem; their solution is to put more money into the 401(k). And, typically, the plan advisor will not fix the problem, particularly if they are paid a commission on each dollar that goes into the 401(k). The 401(k) system is broken—it is not producing healthy retirement outcomes—

---
[7] Gallup Poll, 2014.

but it cannot fix itself. Service providers are incentivized to increase plan assets, not to eliminate personal debt, so there is a conflict of interest. The plan fiduciary advisor *may* be able to provide a solution if they are paid a flat fee rather than a percentage of plan assets (removing the conflicts of interest),[8] but most Recordkeepers cannot provide a solution—they will not tell broke people to get their financial house in order before contributing. The system cannot be fixed from within, and your financial wellness solution will almost certainly need to come from a third-party provider, but which wellness solution fits?

If you want to design a purpose-driven 401(k) that serves your people, you may need to implement a financial wellness program.

EVALUATING FINANCIAL WELLNESS SOLUTIONS[9]

As you know, your company is different, and your employ-

---

[8] Some plan fiduciary advisors are also financial wellness consultants, and some 401(k) specialists have indeed incorporated best practices from financial wellness into their practice. The point is that there is a fundamental conflict of interest if the employee needs to build an emergency fund and eliminate debt and create margin in their life before maximizing their 401(k) contributions, but the 401(k) advisor is only paid on the 401(k) contributions. In other words, the advisor will probably advise them to skip the first few steps and jump to making contributions, even if it is not in the best interest of the plan participant.

[9] In this section, we will evaluate a variety of third-party financial wellness providers. The names of actual financial wellness providers are mentioned for illustration purposes and are neither meant to be inclusive of all providers for each various style nor meant to be an endorsement of the providers named herein. I will broadly recommend certain styles over other styles, but I do not endorse any one provider, as each employer should evaluate the needs of their particular employee population to find the best fit.

ees are unique. Understanding your company culture and each of the styles of solutions helps you identify the best fit. It is not one size fits all, and there may not be a single right answer for your company—there may be several good choices today, or there may be one for now and a different one for later, as needs change.

But if employees are not retiring on time with adequate savings, if they are opting out of your efforts for auto-enrollment and auto-increases, or if preretirement distributions and loans are common, *some* form of financial wellness program is needed. Start with your reasons for even offering employee benefits, and that should lead you to the solution that would support those benefits.

It is hard to imagine a scenario where every company could not benefit from some type of financial wellness engagement. The question is, Which program fits your business?

Generally speaking, there are five broad categories of financial wellness styles. They are listed below in order of value and efficacy, from least valuable to most valuable.

The first style is "**Enhanced Retirement Education**." This constitutes a repackaging from the Recordkeeper of education materials, renamed "financial wellness" to address the growing popularity and demand. Why hire a third-party provider if your Recordkeeper can deliver financial wellness?

Why? Because it is insane to continue doing the same thing and expecting different results. Retirement education alone does not work, and repackaging the lessons as financial wellness does not change their efficacy. Retirement education has largely failed, as too many employees opt out of the auto-features under the economic pressure of decades of poor money management.

Enhanced Retirement Education is the cheapest option, but it is also the least effective.

The second style is "**Products and Services.**" Like the first style, it is also inexpensive, but the reason it is cheap (or free) is because the education may come with a sales pitch. When an insurance company provides financial wellness, it may provide good education about money, but the aim is to sell insurance. It may allow you to provide a low-cost wellness solution for your employees, but it may be in exchange for cross-selling other products. Goldman Sachs sponsors a solution called Ayco to provide financial counseling. Some of the topics covered in their education include wealth transfer and estate planning, and their investment tools are provided as a solution for high-net-worth employees.

This approach may fit for your company and may be more affordable for your employees, but you should understand if products or services are sold in the wellness solution.

The third style is "**Financial Literacy Education.**" It, too, can be a relatively cost-effective solution, but it lacks the sales pitch of the previous style. One example would be EverFi™ Financial Literacy. Another example is Khan Academy, where the lessons and videos are low cost or completely free. The drawback of this third style is that it only works for an employee group that is already highly motivated to seek out and digest the material. In one sense, Financial Literacy Education works best if the population is already fairly...literate. If employees are highly educated and highly motivated, this self-paced approach works well. But some employees need more hand-holding.

The fourth style is called simply "**Tools.**" It is cost-effective for the highly motivated and tech-savvy employee. The Tools are generally web-based. If you want to provide Tools for your employees to build a budget and manage money, there are a variety of providers, including Mint by Intuit and HelloWallet.

In conversations with a Fortune 500 company about financial wellness, we learned they were ready to reject the entire idea of wellness because they had tried (and failed) to implement a program. They had a financial wellness program "nobody used," according to their HR director. The solution they had tried was HelloWallet. They purchased a tool that works well for some companies, but their employees needed a hands-on approach. They needed some education and coaching. Knowing your employees is key to knowing the style that fits.

The fifth style is called "**Behavioral Coaching**." It combines some of the previous styles and is more robust, but may also carry the biggest price tag. The flagship providers in this arena are Enrich, Financial Finesse, and SmartDollar. They provide education, plus tools to help budget, plus an element of coaching. And the individual coaching is shaped around behavioral modification because the numbers change when people change. The bad money habits were developed over years, and it will take time to retrain and break old habits.

Financial Finesse, founded in 1999 by Liz Davidson, is one of the oldest and most highly respected programs. SmartDollar, from Dave Ramsey, is newer. It is the corporate version of the popular Financial Peace University (FPU) program, though SmartDollar is more affordable than FPU and is offered as an employer-sponsored benefit.

Five different styles for you to choose from and multiple vendors within each style. The one you pick depends on your culture. Your 401(k) architect can help you identify the best fit or help you find a financial wellness consultant to find the best fit.

> **THE FIVE STYLES OF FINANCIAL WELLNESS**
>
> 1. Enhanced Retirement Education
>
> 2. Products and Services
>
> 3. Financial Literacy Education
>
> 4. Tools
>
> 5. Behavioral Coaching

With my background in behavioral psychology, you might suspect I favor Behavioral Coaching, but that style may not fit you. It may be cost-prohibitive, and your employees may not need as much hand-holding. Each of the various styles has its merit, all except repackaging retirement education that did not work the first time and expecting it to work now because we call it financial wellness.

A HEALTHY CULTURE MAINTAINS YOUR HEALTHY 401(K)

401(k) architecture designed a plan that serves your purpose and your people, but addressing financial wellness provides the context for your purpose-driven plan to thrive.

Do not make the mistake of skipping over the culture piece and ignoring financial wellness. If cost is a deterrent, you may have to avoid Behavioral Coaching, but the other styles provide affordable alternatives.

I assume if you read this far, you lead a purpose-driven company striving to balance purpose and people and profits. Do not miss the correlation between a great 401(k) and holistic wellness. And please address the culture of wellbeing, or there may be elements of unhealthiness brewing (even if presymptomatic).

Financial wellness must work if the 401(k) is going to work.

And your employees are counting on you to make it work.

CONCLUSION

WEATHERPROOFING TO PREPARE FOR THE NEXT STORM

In conclusion, I would like to celebrate because we survived the storm and to provide some final tips on preparing for the next storm. The year 2020 was a stress test for some, a fire drill for others, a transition for many of us, and (hopefully) a paradigm shift for all of us. Weatherproofing and ongoing maintenance will prepare you (and your employees) for continued success.

Doomsday advocates promoting apocalyptic scenarios were given ample fodder for discussion in 2020.

In January, wildfires consumed large portions of Australia.

In February, locusts consumed parts of Africa.

In March, the COVID-19 pandemic consumed the entire world.

In April, millions were quarantined with stay-at-home orders.

By May, murder hornets appeared in the US.

In June, mass protests that started in Minneapolis swept the globe.

In July, a three-mile-wide comet was barreling toward Earth.

In August, a massive explosion shattered Beirut.

In September, wildfires ravaged California and Oregon.

In October, the Cameron Peak fire became the largest wildfire in Colorado history.

In November, the presidential elections further divided a partisan landscape.

And by December, the coronavirus had changed our planet.

It was a hard year, and few would have been surprised if 2020 had ended with a zombie apocalypse or alien invasion. Almost nothing would have surprised us after a year like this.

The year 2020 was a stress test: a test of our core values and a test of our worldview. Would we continue to live up to those values when things were difficult? Would the test reveal that we operate with an abundance mentality or a scarcity mentality?

This book is about building a 401(k) plan for your employees. But as I interviewed business leaders known for taking care of their employees, it was hard to *just* focus on retirement plans. I found myself writing a book about purpose-driven businesses that care for their people. The key is really about having the right heart for our employees, understanding that people matter, valuing human resources as our most valuable resource, and using the tools to express that sentiment.

The 401(k) plan is just one of those tools, although it may be one of the most important pieces of the foundation. According to the Investment Company Institute, 401(k) plans held $6.2 trillion in assets as of December 31, 2019, on behalf of more than 58 million active participants and tens of millions of former employees. Simply put, a lot of hardworking Americans are counting on us to get this right.

So, yes, this is a how-to book for employers on how to

provide this cornerstone benefit, but it must be set in the context of what Ron Hill called "conscious capitalism," and it must fit within what Anne St. Peter called "the balance between purpose and profit."

The year 2020 was a stress test of our purpose. It was harder to balance purpose and profits and people, but those who did, did well.

The year 2020 was a fire drill: survival instincts (and fear) ruled the day. Would we abandon long-term planning for short-term goals? Would we solve long-term problems with short-term solutions? The shorter our focus, the more stressed we became. When the fire drill sounded, some only heard one message: "Get out!"

And, indeed, the crisis was extreme for millions of Americans, many who died and many others who lost jobs. Sean Kouplen said, "We had an Oklahoma Business Relief Program that I put together at the state level, and we went through $100 million in business relief in $25,000 grants in eight hours. In the second phase, we went through $50 million in only an hour. To qualify, you had to be a small business with revenue down 25% year-over-year, and tons of companies in our state qualified. The demand was overwhelming."

The year 2020 was a year of transition, with changes

in how we work and live. Anxiety and stress (particularly financial stress) were high, even for normal people, even for those who did not lose their jobs. Having lived through 2020, it felt like we were living through history, like today's headlines might be something studied and analyzed for hundreds of years. As I said in the introduction, "paradigm shift" did not seem adequate to describe the changes occurring. Maybe the changes will be in how we treat employees.

The leaders of successful businesses find ways to communicate that they care, or they eventually forfeit their share... in that company's success. It may not be immediate, the collapse and degradation may be slow, but businesses that do not value their people will eventually lose value. The paycheck is not the reward; it is the fulfillment of a contractual obligation. The reward is the care, the love, the employee benefits, the fringe benefits, and the pats on the back. The reward is what they call "lagniappe" in Louisiana—the giving of "a little something extra"—that separates successful businesses from all of the rest.

I hope and pray that 2020 enacted the real change it appears to have brought, that we never treat money the same, that we never treat our employees the same, and that we never treat one another the same. I am not naïve. I realize that there is an economic purpose for business that trumps any altruistic efforts to treat employees like family. But my point is that these are not mutually exclusive. Businesses must be profitable, but taking care of your employees (valuing them and loving them) is a means to that end.

There are a variety of ways to tell our people they matter, but one of the easiest ways is through the employee benefits program. And when our employees cross the finish line, they will appreciate that *they* worked at a place where the 401(k) also worked.

Sean Kouplen of Regent Bank talked about that little something extra that employees can give when they know you care. That little something extra is the difference between being ordinary and extraordinary, between being conventional in business and unconventional, between surviving and thriving.

In a tough year like 2020, those who cared, fared…they fared better. They did not just survive; they thrived.

And yet the uncomfortable questions I found myself asking are "How do we help leaders care? How do we change the hearts of those who have been entrusted with the care of others?"

I believe a business case can be built to support the value of love and care in the workplace, that employee benefits costing dollars and cents really do make sense. The stress test of 2020 provided evidence that living up to our values was not in spite of the difficulties but actually a means of surviving and thriving during those difficulties. Maybe seeing the evidence for success under such challenging conditions changed a few minds about corporate responsibility. But did it change any hearts?

Beyond the empirical evidence, we must ask how our hearts are working. After all, 2020 was more than just a test of these values; 2020 was also a test of how our hearts work.

During the interviews I conducted for this book, I asked business leaders how hearts are changed, and specifically what changed their hearts and motivated them to aspire to better corporate values. Some said that they were motivated by seeing business done really poorly when they were young, and they aspired to something better, but most said they were motivated by the stories of others who were doing it better, business leaders doing so much good in the world. Here in Kansas City, for instance, the investments by Henry W. Bloch of H&R Block and Don Hall of Hallmark Cards are inspiring. Others were inspired by the story of Jim Stowers, who founded American Century and then, after he and his wife both had cancer, started the Stowers Institute for Medical Research, finding a way to have the profits from American Century fund the efforts to find a cure. Others were inspired by Patagonia and all that they are doing to make certain that the world is still here for our children and grandchildren, or Ben & Jerry's ice cream and how they are working, with every scoop, to make the world a better place.

Patagonia and Ben & Jerry's are both B Corps, along with Global Prairie, and I would have to say that it was extremely inspiring interviewing these business leaders for the book. My hope and prayer is that you were as inspired by reading their stories as I was in first hearing them. The idea of Global Prairie voluntarily giving back so much of their profits, or the idea of Jericho Home Improvement taking care of the orphan and abandoned child. It seems like bad business advice until you realize these entities are much richer for their investments, that as they enrich their community, there is a direct return on investments.

Christopher Marquis, who taught for 10 years at Harvard Business School and is now a professor in sustainable global enterprise at Cornell University, is the author of *Better Business: How the B Corp Movement Is Remaking Capitalism*. Thanks to Anne St. Peter, Dr. Marquis was in Kansas City recently, along with the CEO of Patagonia, the CEO of H&R Block, and the CEO of Hallmark to discuss purpose-oriented businesses in the heartland. In the Midwest, CEOs show up, they care about the community, they care about their employees, and they want to make a difference. It appears to be a global movement that more and more businesses are asking the questions about how they can make a positive change. I am hopeful that stories like those included in this book might fuel this initiative.

As Anne St. Peter, the co-founder of Global Prairie, put it, "I was so motivated by those corporate stories that I said, 'I want to run a company like that.' And I think you are either a business leader who somehow believes that business can be a force for good and get turned on by stories—those unique individuals who get turned on by all aspects of a rich life and weave it into business that the world needs. I think post-COVID, if we can't emerge from this earth-shattering shock to our system and not realize that business needs to be changed for good, more heart and more care, more community, more kindness, that we need to see each other more. And we need to work together, and we need to be more present, more understanding of one another. There's a way to do business better post-COVID, I think with more heart and more understanding, and I think a book like this is needed."

WEATHERPROOFING AND ONGOING MAINTENANCE

For many of us, 2020 was a stress test—a fire drill. For some it was hell. For most it was like a hailstorm.

Most (not all, but most) businesses will survive the hailstorm, but there will be hail damage to repair, and we must weatherproof our financial house in preparation for the next storm. The year 2020 underscored the need for ongoing maintenance.

Living in the Midwest, we are all too familiar with spring storms that bring tornadoes and hail. Fortunately, the tornadoes are isolated events, (typically) cutting a narrow path of destruction while leaving others untouched only a block away. The pandemic was like this—leveling one business but missing the next. There are some who live their entire lives in the Midwest, hearing tornado sirens every spring but never actually seeing a tornado. The hail, however, is more prevalent, whether it is large hailstones that cause extensive damage or small hailstones that wear out roofs over time. And the pandemic was like this, too, impacting everyone.

A best practice for your business (and your 401k) is to weatherproof the financial house with a covering of financial wellness. And I do not just mean having a financial wellness program, although a formal financial wellness program is beneficial; I mean underscoring strategic decisions with the principles of holistic financial wellness.

Charles Casteel, the CFO of Phenix Label Company, said they learned this principle the hard way. A storm hit their business in 2008—dual tornadoes with the Recession and a lawsuit—and they leveraged themselves quite a bit to defend the business while weathering a down market. It took years for them to recover, but, as Casteel put it, "Once we got all of that debt paid off, we decided to never put ourselves in that position again."

Listeners often call the popular radio broadcast of *The Ramsey Show* to exclaim their new status as "debt-free!" but the CEO of Phenix Label has a sign on his office door that makes the same proclamation.

Individuals who were debt-free and businesses that were not heavily leveraged weathered the storm of 2020 differently. What might seem like an acceptable business practice under normal economic conditions can prove disastrous when the clouds gather. Kouplen noted that his companies have zero debt. "And when we don't have any debt," he said, "you can have a ton of flexibility." Harris Rosen experienced the same thing. His company's value was loving people, but his company's position as debt-free allowed them the flexibility to put that into action.

If the business is grounded in the principles of financial wellness, it is easier to bring the 401(k) plan under the same umbrella for the employees. Helping your employees put their financial house in order does not start with putting more money in the 401(k); it starts with teaching the principles of stewardship, budgeting, and eliminating debt, which ultimately frees up the resources to put more money in the 401(k).

The 401(k) plan should be offered as part of a holistic financial wellness program—not the other way around. The financial wellness program is not merely an education course within the 401(k); it is foundational to providing a 401(k). Think of it as weatherproofing the roof before the next storm. (Because there will be more storms in your future.)

And ongoing maintenance is vital to regular upkeep to maintain the integrity of the structure. This means benchmarking services and fees annually, monitoring the fiduciaries of your plan, and taking the plan out to bid every three to five years, which might include a formal RFP process.

In the retirement plan industry, a Request for Proposal (RFP) was a standard process for large institutional plans, but over the years, this practice has become more prevalent in the mid to large market space (shifting from plans of more than $100 million in assets to plans of only $20 million or less). There are few standardized methods, however, and most RFPs we receive illustrate the confusion.

It is not prudent for you if unfamiliar with such matters to write your own RFP, facilitate or manage the RFP process, or evaluate responses to the RFP. Best practices would recommend having a third party facilitate the RFP.

Employers who are unwilling to pay the cost for this project may not be in a position to issue an RFP. (Quite frankly, some RFPs are issued from companies that are too small to do a formal RFP.) You can find a third-party professional to run the project for you at retirementadvisor.us/advisor-search-top.

Every 401(k) plan should evaluate service providers on at least an annual basis. (Investments should be evaluated quarterly, but service providers should be evaluated annually.) This assumes you have a Retirement Plan Committee—that you did not skip the first step in designing the 401(k)—and this assumes an established pattern of evaluation with fees and services.

Every three to five years, this process should include soliciting bids from other service providers (that is, from other Recordkeepers and administrators). This can be done as a "blind bid" without current service providers knowing they are being evaluated and without other service providers knowing on whom they are bidding. The plan fiduciary advisor should be fully capable of facilitating this process without the need of a formal RFP. If, however, the bidding process indicates that a formal RFP would be beneficial, this is an easy project to transition to. By the way, an RFP to benchmark the Recordkeeper and administrator is technically a "limited-scope" RFP, something most plan fiduciary advisors can do at no additional cost.

Periodically, you may need to do a full-scope RFP, meaning

an evaluation of all service providers, including advisory services. This type of RFP should be conducted by an independent agent, and you should be willing to pay for this project. The independent agent could be an ERISA attorney or an independent Certified Plan Fiduciary Advisor (CPFA®) who evaluates the plan and provides solutions without offering their own services as part of that solution (which would be a conflict of interest). It is worth paying an independent party to get this right.

The correct way to do an RFP is to search for the plan fiduciary advisor first and then work with this plan fiduciary advisor to identify the correct Recordkeeper and administrator. Sometimes the employer drafts the RFP, sends it out to a dozen or more advisors, and asks them to bring a "bundled" solution (meaning each advisor is supposed to bring one Recordkeeper and/or one administrator). The questions in the RFP are confusing—it is not clear whether they pertain to the advisor or the Recordkeeper—because the author of the RFP was confused. Of the dozen or so respondents, some may bring the same Recordkeeper, which complicates the situation further.

Should we hire advisor A, who brought Recordkeeper X and administrator N?

Should we hire advisor B, who brought Recordkeeper Y and no third-party administrator?

Or should we hire advisor C, who brought Recordkeeper Z?

What if the committee favored advisor C but Recordkeeper Y and administrator N? Most committees have no idea what they need, what they are looking for, or how to properly evaluate the differences.

Best practices for an RFP would suggest the following model:

- You hire a CPFA® to conduct the RFP.
- The CPFA® interviews you and writes the RFP.
- The CPFA® issues the RFP to other advisors.
- The CPFA® solicits responses and interviews respondents.
- The CPFA® and committee meet with advisors A, B, and C. (The CPFA® does *not* offer their own proposal as advisor D. This would be a conflict of interest.)
- Once the committee selects the plan advisor, you work together to bring a recordkeeping solution.

The point is that regular maintenance is required, those with the expertise must be involved in the process, and employers benefit from paying for a professional to get this right.

Our employees are counting on us to get it right, and the next storm (or test) could be right around the corner.

LAGNIAPPE: ADDING "A LITTLE SOMETHING EXTRA"

My hope, as Anne St. Peter put it, is that we emerge from this earth-shattering storm as better versions of ourselves, as better people with better businesses, with more heart and more care.

And my prayer is that readers have been inspired to care.

If you are a business leader who strives to give "a little something extra," I am confident that you will receive the same and more—lagniappe—from your people.

I welcome questions and comments about your efforts to lead a purpose-driven business and care for your employees. Are you part of the B Corp movement? Are you interested in having a business that makes a greater impact for good? Let's start a dialogue. Email me directly: troy@PHDfirm.com.

ACKNOWLEDGMENTS

- This book is intended for informational and educational purposes only and is intended to be general in nature. As your investment or retirement circumstances may be unique, you should seek personalized advice that is customized for your particular situation. This general information is not intended to be financial advice, legal advice, or tax advice for your personal circumstances.
- Throughout the book, particularly in Chapter 1, I include the results of multiple interviews with successful business leaders about the ROI of taking care of their employees and investing in employee benefits. The business leaders interviewed were selected based upon workplace ratings as top employers in their industry and may or may not be clients of PHD. Retirement Consulting. Their inclusion in this book is not an endorsement by the author of their businesses. Similarly, these inter-

views may not be considered an endorsement by these businesses of the author or of the advisory practice of PHD. Consulting, and as these businesses may not be clients of the author, their quotes may not be considered testimonials.
- Photographs of the author: Linsey McAfee.
- And my heartfelt gratitude to a team of editors and friends who provided invaluable feedback throughout this process, first from within my inner circle and eventually with the team at Houndstooth. Thanks to Kristalynn and Neddie Ann. Could not have done this without you.
- Investment advisory services provided by PHD. Retirement Consulting, a Registered Investment Adviser. Noninvestment consulting services provided by PHD. Consulting, LLC, a separate entity. The firm provides Fee-Only Retirement Plan Consulting and Financial Wellness. More information may be found at **FeeOnly401kAdvisor.com**.

ABOUT THE AUTHOR

TROY REDSTONE is a Fee-Only retirement plan consultant, an accomplished public speaker and published author, and Behavioral Finance expert. He designs and manages financial wellness programs and ERISA employer-sponsored retirement plans (401k, 403b, Governmental 457 plans). He is a Certified Plan Fiduciary Advisor (CPFA®), a Certified Behavioral Finance Analyst (CBFA®), a Certified Financial Education Instructor (CFEI®), and an Accredited Investment Fiduciary (AIF®).

As the founder of PHD. Retirement Consulting, he helps employees retire better and helps employers sleep better. Known as "The Dave Ramsey of 401(k)s," he's passionate about promoting financial wellness through retirement plans and encouraging employees to eliminate debt and practice good stewardship.

He is a member of the **Retirement Advisor Council**, recognized as one of the 125 leaders in the retirement plan industry in America, and currently serves as the President (2018–2021) as well as Chairman of the Board for the **Employee Benefits Institute** (2019). He is a thought-leader in the retirement plan industry and a 30-year veteran of keynote speaking at conferences and seminars throughout the country.

This is his second book. His first book was the bestseller *Repurposement: Experiencing the Financial Freedom to Start Living on Purpose Today*. He attended the University of Alabama (Behavioral Psychology and Journalism), Anderson University (MDiv), and Rockhurst University (Finance).

He lives in Kansas City with his bride of 26 years, an Aussiedoodle named Dixie Belle, and occasionally his daughter and son, when home from college.

REFERENCES

Benartzi, S. (2012). *Save more tomorrow*. Penguin.

Bible, New International Version.

Bible, New King James Version.

Bible, The Message Version.

Blanchett, D. M., & Grantz, J. E. (2011). Retirement success: A surprising look into the factors that drive positive outcomes. *ASPA Journal*, *41*(3). https://www.asppa.org/sites/asppa.org/files/PDFs/Magazines/ASPPA%20Journal/TAJ-Summer2011-ret-success.pdf

Center for Systems Science and Engineering. (2021). *COVID-19 dashboard*. Johns Hopkins University and Medicine. https://coronavirus.jhu.edu/map.html

EACH Enterprise. (2014). *The value of a professional retirement plan advisor*.

El-Erian, M. (2020, March 20). *Squawk box*. CNBC.

Elton, E. J., Gruber, M. J., DeSouza, A., & Blake, C. R. (2017). *Target date funds: What's under the hood?* Center for Retirement Research at Boston College.

Employee Retirement Income Security Act of 1974. Pub.L. 93–406, 88 Stat. 829, enacted September 2, 1974, codified in part at 29 U.S.C. ch. 18.

Freidman, Z. (2019, January 11). 78% of workers live paycheck to paycheck. *Forbes.* https://www.forbes.com/sites/zackfriedman/2019/01/11/live-paycheck-to-paycheck-government-shutdown/?sh=62834f5d4f10

Hacobian, C. (2018, June 27). Here's how high planes actually fly, according to experts. *Time.* https://time.com/5309905/how-high-do-planes-fly/#:~:text=Commercial%20aircraft%20typically%20fly%20between,a%20flight%2C%20according%20to%20Beckman.&text=And%20the%20weight%20of%20the%20plane%20changes%20as,climbs%20higher%20into%20the%20sky

Hellmich, N. (2014, March 18). Retirement: A third have less than $1,000 put away. *USA Today.* https://www.usatoday.com/story/money/personalfinance/2014/03/18/retirement-confidence-survey-savings/6432241/

Is your state making the grade? (2017). Champlain College. https://www.champlain.edu/centers-of-experience/center-for-financial-literacy/report-national-high-school-financial-literacy

Kelly, J. (2020, August 20). Jobless claims: 57.4 million Americans have sought unemployment benefits since mid-March—Over 1 million people filed last week. *Forbes.* https://www.forbes.com/sites/jackkelly/2020/08/20/jobless-claims-574-million-americans-have-sought-unemployment-benefits-since-mid-marchover-1-million-people-filed-last-week/?sh=7fe8acb96d59

Redstone, T. (2019). *Repurposement: Experiencing the financial freedom to start living on purpose today.* Mahout Press.

Restrepo, T., & Shuford, H. (2011). *Workers compensation and the aging workforce*. National Council on Compensation Insurance.

Retirement Advisor Council. (2021). *Research report: Advisors take steps to measure employee engagement in financial wellness programs*. https://www.retirementadvisor.us/report-2021

Rosenbaum, A. (2019, June 14). *Surely, you need an ERISA attorney* [Conference presentation]. 401(k) Conference. Denver, CO.

Sanders, K. (Interviewer). (2020, April 1). *NBC nightly news*. NBC.

The six dimensions of wellness. (2020). National Wellness Institute. https://nationalwellness.org/resources/six-dimensions-of-wellness/

Thaler, R. (2015). *Misbehaving: The making of behavioral economics*. Norton.

Employee Benefits Security Administration. (2013). *Target date retirement funds—Tips for ERISA plan fiduciaries*. US Department of Labor.

Van Harlow, W. (2012, August 27). Defined contribution plans: Missing the forest for the trees? *Financial Advisor*. https://www.fa-mag.com/news/defined-contribution-plans-missing-the-forest-for-the-trees-11709.html

Wells, L. (2020, November 9). *What is the best debt-to-income ratio for a mortgage?* Bankrate. https://www.bankrate.com/mortgages/why-debt-to-income-matters-in-mortgages/

CPSIA information can be obtained
at www.ICGtesting.com
Printed in the USA
BVHW081528051121
620610BV00003B/9/J